Battle Orders • 23

Desert Raiders: Axis and Allied Special Forces 1940–43

Andrea Molinari

Consultant Editor Dr Duncan Anderson • *Series editors* Marcus Cowper and Nikolai Bogdanovic

First published in Great Britain in 2007 by Osprey Publishing,
Midland House, West Way, Botley, Oxford OX2 0PH, UK
44-02 23rd St, Suite 219, Long Island City, NY 11101, USA
Email: info@ospreypublishing.com

Transferred to digital print on demand 2010

First published 2007
3rd impression 2008

Printed and bound by PrintOnDemand-Worldwide.com, Peterborough, UK

A CIP catalogue record for this book is available from the British Library

ISBN: 978 1 84603 006 2

Editorial by Ilios Publishing Ltd, Oxford, UK (www.iliospublishing.com)
Page layout by Bounford.com, Huntingdon, UK
Index by Alan Thatcher
Typeset in Gill Sans and Stone Serif
Originated by United Graphics, Singapore

Author's note

This is a collective work that could be written only thanks to the efforts of many contributors: Luca Pastori, Carlo Pecchi, Antonio Attarantato,
Stephan Ferrand and, especially, Pier Paolo Battistelli, whose help and friendship made everything possible. The author is very grateful
also to Piero Crociani and Filippo Cappellano, who provided precious help as well as the original documents held by the Italian Army Archive
used to outline the development of the Italian and Libyan forces employed for the defence of the Sahara.

Imperial War Museum collections

Many of the photos in this book come from the Imperial War Museum's huge collections that cover all aspects of conflict involving Britain
and the Commonwealth since the start of the 20th century. These rich resources are available online to search, browse and buy at
www.iwmcollections.org.uk. In addition to Collections Online, you can visit the Visitor Rooms where you can explore over 8 million photographs,
thousands of hours of moving images, the largest sound archive of its kind in the world, thousands of diaries and letters written by people in
wartime, and a huge reference library. To make an appointment, call (020) 7416 5320, or email: mail@iwm.org.uk.
Im\perial War Museum www.iwm.org.uk

Cover image E21338 © IWM.

The Woodland Trust

Osprey Publishing is supporting the Woodland Trust, the UK's leading woodland conservation charity, by funding the dedication of trees.

www.ospreypublishing.com

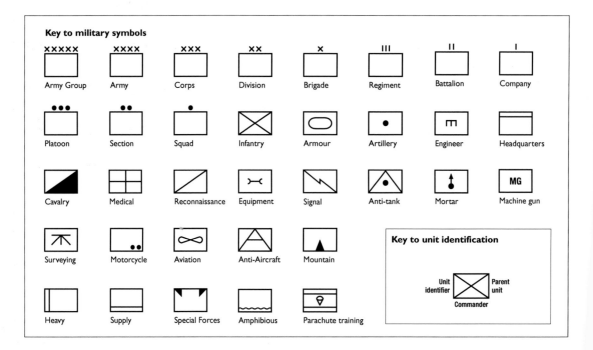

Contents

Introduction   4

Combat mission   6

Doctrine and training   9

Unit organization   14
British forces • Italian forces • Free French forces • German forces

Tactics   50
The LRDG in the Fezzan, 27 December 1940–9 February 1941 • The Free French at Kufra, February 1941
Reconnaissance in Cyrenaica and Tripolitania • The first campaign in the Fezzan, February–March 1942
The LRDG/SAS partnership, March–May 1942 • The big raids, September 1942
The raids in Egypt, July–August 1942

Command, control, communications and intelligence (C3I)   76
Command • Control • Communications • Intelligence

Weapons and equipment   82
Weapons • Vehicles and equipment

Lessons learned   88
Interaction with the environment

Chronology   90

Bibliography   92

Glossary   93

Index   95

Introduction

Between June 1940 and January 1943 Italian, German, British, Commonwealth, Indian and French troops struggled for control of the Western Desert, their battles being primarily fought in the Libyan province of Cyrenaica and Western Egypt. What is known as the 'Desert War' was actually fought in a relatively narrow strip close to the shores of the Mediterranean Sea due to the difficulties of supply and movement in a desert zone.

But several hundred kilometres to the south, deep in the vast inner desert area known as the Sahara, one of the driest and most inhospitable regions of the world, another desert war was fought, one that might be called the real 'desert' war. This war saw Allied and Axis forces involved in a struggle that bore little resemblance to the major conflict unfolding on the coastal strip.

It was a war that, in its own way, marked the coming of a new style of warfare; a style defined by skilled men bound to their vehicles, men who proved capable of striking well behind enemy lines, men who had to fight against a hostile environment as well as against their enemies. Many lessons were learned during the war, some forgotten, others not. What has not been forgotten, however, is the valour, courage, skill and ingenuity demonstrated by these men during their struggle.

The Italian fort of Bu Ngem, some 300km north of Hon on the road to Misurata. Nearly all the Italian garrisons were accommodated in forts, whose structure was very simple, with rectangular or square outer walls enclosing quarters for the garrison. As they were mostly built in the 1930s, motor vehicles were not usually catered for. The trellis structure is a radio antenna mast. (Piero Crociani)

The difficulties of crossing the desert are amply demonstrated here. The first attempt by von Almaszy to reach the Nile was aborted due to travel difficulties. (Carlo Pecchi)

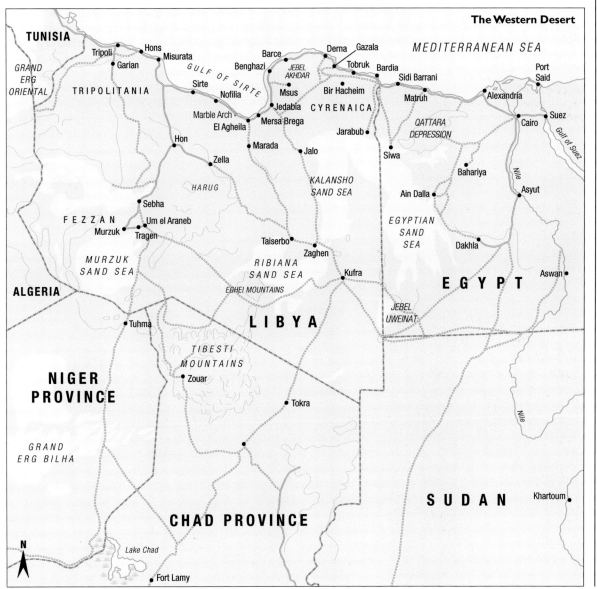

The Western Desert

TUNISIA

MEDITERRANEAN SEA

GRAND ERG ORIENTAL

Tripoli · Hons · Misurata

Garian

TRIPOLITANIA

GULF OF SIRTE

Sirte

Nofilia

Barce · Derna · Gazala

Benghazi · Tobruk · Bardia

JEBEL AKHDAR · Sidi Barrani

Msus · Bir Hacheim · Matruh

Port Said

Alexandria

Cairo · Suez

Gulf of Suez

Marble Arch · Mersa Brega

El Agheila

CYRENAICA

Jarabub

QATTARA DEPRESSION

Hon

Marada · Jalo

Siwa

Bahariya

Nile

Zella

KALANSHO SAND SEA

Ain Dalla

Asyut

HARUG

EGYPTIAN SAND SEA

Sebha

Um el Araneb

FEZZAN

Murzuk · Tragen

MURZUK SAND SEA

Taiserbo

RIBIANA SAND SEA

Zaghen

Kufra

Dakhla

EGYPT

Aswan

EGHEI MOUNTAINS

JEBEL UWEINAT

ALGERIA

Tuhma

L I B Y A

NIGER PROVINCE

TIBESTI MOUNTAINS

Zouar

Tokra

GRAND ERG BILHA

CHAD PROVINCE

S U D A N

Khartoum

Nile

N

Lake Chad

Fort Lamy

Combat mission

A group of Italian officers leading a *Meharisti* unit in the desert. All of them are riding barefoot and wear the *Sahariana*. Their only armament is the 6.5mm Mannlicher Carcano Model 91/24 rifle. (Piero Crociani)

The Libyan Desert is a huge area of more than 3,000,000km^2 stretching for about 1,500km south from the Mediterranean and about 2,000km west from the Nile Valley to the mountains of Tunisia and Algeria. The environment is absolutely inhospitable, with temperatures rising to as high as 60 degrees Centigrade during the day and dropping below zero by night. Water (drawn from artesian wells) can be found only in few oases, where the only vegetation in the area grows. Roads are simply non-existent; what can be found are at best tracks and paths marking the vast plains and depressions. Almost no human being can be found in the huge sand seas of Murzuk, in the Fezzan (as the desert south of Tripoli is called), as well as further to the east in the sand seas of Ribiana and Kalansho, which, along with the Great Sand Sea of Egypt, practically bar the road to eastwards. To the south the Tibesti Mountains, rising up to 3,000m, bar the road to Niger and Chad (the lower heights of Jebel Uweinat also bar the road to the Sudan).

At first glance, such an inhospitable region would appear to have little military value. However, following the surrender of France in June 1940 the Sahara became an attractive area to control. It offered the Italians a chance to disrupt the Takouradi air route through which aircraft were flown in to Egypt. They could also move from Libya across the desert to reach the lower Nile in the Sudan and try to establish a link with their Eastern Africa colonies.

An AS37, modified with a 75mm gun, and an AS42 Sahariana to the rear. The AS37 and AS42 proved very effective vehicles, with good firepower and mobility, and they gave the Italian forces the ability to respond quickly. (Filippo Cappellano – AUSSME)

From the French point of view, as soon as the Free French forces took control of Cameroon and Chad in August 1941, the Sahara offered them the only chance to fight a war on their own against Axis forces in North Africa.

For the British, a single officer, Ralph Bagnold, was able to figure out that the Sahara could provide a useful 'back door' to move behind Italian lines in North Africa and harass their lines of communication. This concept was not entirely new: during World War I another British officer, Thomas Edward Lawrence ('Lawrence of Arabia'), had successfully waged a war behind the Turkish front line. However, while Lawrence waged a guerrilla war with local tribesmen,

An LRDG patrol leaving the Siwa Oasis on 25 May 1942. Siwa was the main base for British raiding and scouting forces. (IWM, E 012375)

Bagnold set out to wage a modern style of warfare reliant upon what would now be called special forces. These forces relied on the ability to travel vast distances unsupported throughout the Saharan wastes, not tied (at least not completely) to the oases, and could therefore operate deep behind enemy lines to gather intelligence and strike at targets, particularly airfields, that had appeared completely secure.

A comparison between the combat mission of the Long Range Desert Group (LRDG) and the other forces operating in the Sahara illustrates the groundbreaking developments introduced by the British unit. The Free French forces partly borrowed the LRDG's means and tactics, but were still bound to the basic concepts of 19th-century colonial warfare. The same was even truer for the Italians who for the first two years of the war only sought to defend their strongpoints. The fact that the Italians, and Germans, belatedly attempted to develop a special forces presence in the Sahara only illustrates how effective the LRDG's tactics had been.

Doctrine and training

European colonial armies in North Africa mostly settled themselves along the coasts and in major towns, rarely venturing into the deep desert. A military presence in the inland regions was established, but only following a defensive pattern. Key positions were the oases, soon turned into fortified positions, which represented the bedrock of the European presence in the desert. These strongholds provided a focal point for garrisons and a shelter for columns and patrols in a way unchanged since Kitchener's campaign in the Sudan that culminated in the battle of Omdurman in 1898. Unlike the local Arab tribes, European armies were bound to slow-moving supply chains that, coupled with the lack of adequate movement capabilities, slowed the pace of movement right down. A suitable solution was found in 'hopping' from one fort to another, a doctrine Kitchener developed by establishing large supply dumps that moved forward with the bulk of the troops. In this way his forces, though still 'hopping' from one oasis to another, could be grouped together in a stronger force than the small columns previously used.

The widespread diffusion of motorization during and after World War I brought a change to the practice of desert warfare. In 1916 British troops had to face a revolt by the Arab Senussi tribe in Libya, where Italian forces only garrisoned the coastal towns. Fast-moving and well-armed armoured cars were used not only to lead the way for regular British forces, but also to perform 'special missions' (like the rescue of the crews of two British ships held by the Senussi), which involved deep penetration into the desert. Most noticeably these armoured cars served with Duke of Westminster's No. 2 Armoured Motor Squadron, whose personnel transferred en bloc from the Navy to the Army and formed up to six light car patrols. Although these patrols never penetrated too deeply into the desert, it is they who are the true antecedents of the LRDG rather than Lawrence and his guerrilla forces in Arabia.

When the Italian Army undertook the 'reconquest' of Libya in the 1930s (actually its first penetration into the deep desert) they made use of a large number of motor vehicles, yet still with a tactical doctrine based on 19th-century colonial principles. Motorized units were still used in the desert in the same manner as fast-moving camel-mounted troops – hopping from one oasis to another and from one stronghold to another.

An interesting feature of Italian defensive organization in the Sahara was the large number of landing strips spread throughout the area. Originally these were intended to host the aircraft of the Aviazione Sahariana, which were mainly used for reconnaissance; they were later used to bring in supplies to remote locations. Here a group of Libyan soldiers unloads supplies from a Savoia Marchetti SM82 Marsupiale somewhere in the desert. (Piero Crociani)

When World War II broke out in the Mediterranean and North Africa, the European armies faced the problem that this time their opponents would not be poorly armed tribesmen, but other modern European forces. The French and Italians stayed true to their 19th-century-style doctrines, which ruled out any chance of effectively waging war in the deep desert. This was a conscious decision as in the vastness of Sahara those who controlled the strongpoints in the oases enjoyed major advantages against any attacker in that they had plenty of water, food and ammunition. Although weapons issued to such posts were often old, they were deemed suitable enough to face the unlikely eventuality of attacks coming from and through the desert. There had been some motorization but not a substantial amount, and the available vehicles were largely unsuitable, either because they lacked cross-country capabilities and reliability, or because their payload was insufficient to carry men, weapons and all the supplies needed.

Although the Italians now faced very different enemies to the Senussi tribesmen they had fought in the 1930s, they simply improved their old doctrines rather than seeking any new solutions. Shortly before Italy's entry into war, the staff led by the Governor of Libya elaborated the directives for the defence of the colony in the case of, particularly, a French attack from Tunisia that might outflank their border defences. Their strategy relied heavily on static troops tied to strongpoints, though they were also assigned the role of carrying out sudden attacks against enemy bases and supply columns; true 'mobile' warfare was only left to the five 'sahariana' companies, whose task was to take the war into enemy territory.

Given this tactical situation, Ralph Bagnold's concepts were inventive and innovative. Surprisingly, behind them lay a gross overestimation of the capabilities of the Italian forces in the area. Bagnold had encountered the Italian Auto-Saharan during his travels in the desert, and warned the British staff in Egypt that, as soon as it entered war, Italy could start large-scale actions using 'light mobile forces in desert cars' in the Libyan–Egyptian desert. The aim of these attacks would be to divert British attention from the main front, as well as to carry out special operations such as the sabotage and harassment of the British lines of communications, or even to establish landing grounds in the desert and bring agents and supplies for the many pro-Fascist Italians then

Three Libyans in the most typical defensive position in the desert: a hole dug in the sand. The one at centre mans a 6.5mm Breda 30 light machine gun; this weapon was very complex and prone to jam. The cradle on the left contained 72 O.T.O. Model 35 hand grenades. (Piero Crociani)

living in Egypt. The fall of France in June 1940 made the picture even gloomier: now the Italians could easily move to the south and the south-east, threatening the Takouradi air route and even linking up with their forces in East Africa, a move that would endanger the British position in Sudan. Though completely devoid of any basis in reality, these evaluations offer a clear perspective of the motives behind the LRDG's doctrine for desert warfare. Rather than limiting themselves to hopping from one oasis to another in the attempt to establish advanced bases from which carry out their missions, Bagnold's LRDG was to perform long-range missions penetrating deeply into the desert and well behind the enemy lines. This wasn't simply a modernization of guerrilla tactics used in the Sahara for centuries, as the LRDG wasn't bound to a specific territory or tribe. Bagnold relied on modern means: reliable vehicles, smart equipment, good weaponry and an original approach to desert navigation.

Although the LRDG was born with the aim of preventing Italian long-range activities in the desert, it soon devoted itself to offensive capabilities, either carrying out long-range reconnaissance missions ('road watching') or performing acts of sabotage and harassment behind enemy lines. Despite this change of direction, the focus of the LRDG remained fixed on its ability to function in the desert: not only fulfilling its assigned tasks but, above all, learning and perfecting the skills necessary to survive in such a dry and inhospitable region. Unsurprisingly, training focussed on survival skills, navigation and the ability to repair any damaged or broken-down vehicles; in addition to this specific technical skills like wireless communications were vital. A look at the breakdown of specializations in the LRDG is revealing. According to the November 1940 war establishment, each LRDG patrol (comprising one captain, one subaltern, one staff sergeant and 27 other ranks)

A *Meharisti* group setting up a temporary camp close to an oasis in the desert. The men arrived, unsaddled their camels and had a brief meal gathered in small groups, while one of them kept watch. Afterwards, in the heat of the day, they rested before resuming their march. One of the main drawbacks camel-mounted units faced when compared with motorized ones was their lightweight armament, which can clearly be seen here. (Piero Crociani)

should include one Royal Army Ordnance Corps (RAOC) fitter and one driver/mechanic, two navigators, two gunners, 14 drivers and only seven general-duty men. These percentages remained unchanged in 1942, when a single patrol (comprising one officer, one warrant officer or sergeant, and 13 other ranks) was made of one driver/mechanic, one navigator, two gunners, seven drivers and only two general-duty men.

The flexibility of the LRDG led to further developments in late 1941 when it began a fruitful cooperation with the Special Air Squadron (then 'L' Detachment), which developed into relationships with the various other Allied special forces operating in the region – Commandos (both European and Arab), 'Folboats' and various kinds of intelligence agent. The joint LRDG/SAS missions proved the potential of deep desert penetration warfare: targets could be reached well behind enemy lines, either for sabotage or reconnaissance purposes; enemy patrols could easily be avoided whilst the oasis-based strongpoints became obsolete.

From late 1941 improved Italian leadership brought about some changes in doctrine: camel-mounted units were reduced in number and strength while well-armed, fully motorized patrols were formed. Mobile patrols were now intended to cover wider areas from their fixed strongpoints, and they had to effectively fight against enemy units, not just to discover where they were. Also, soon after the end of the spring 1942 campaign, the Italians made a coherent attempt to improve their defences. Motorization acquired a greater importance, and more and better armed *Compagnie Sahariane* were formed. These units were kept active in the areas most likely to see enemy activity, with the aim of discovering their whereabouts and fixing them in place until reinforcements could be summoned. This was the first step to developing a doctrine for desert warfare clearly based upon the LRDG example. Between summer and autumn 1942 the Italians set up their own deep raiding patrols and, belatedly, they could rely both on adequate vehicles (the AS42 Sahariana, the only vehicle of the war designed specifically for this kind of activity) and men (the newly formed Arditi companies) with which to successfully harass British the rear area.

Below and opposite: two photographs, probably staged or taken during a drill, of a group of Libyan *Meharisti* in the desert. They show how the camel-mounted troops were trained to fight when they encountered the enemy. Once they left their camels they ran towards the intended position. The most favourable position was behind a sand dune where they could remain unseen until the enemy approached before breaking from cover to fire from the top of it. With the exception of a single man carrying a 6.5mm Breda 30 machine gun, all the *Meharisti* are armed with the 6.5mm 91/24 rifle or the 91/38 musket. These photographs show how practical the typical baggy Arab trousers (called *Siroual*) were, both for riding a camel or running in the desert. (Piero Crociani)

These improvements helped the Italians to counter the threat posed by the Free French in spring 1942. Another factor that helped was the Free French's limited improvement of their own doctrine. Leclerc's forces had a good desert-crossing capability, but lacked strength in terms of numbers and weapons, so they restricted themselves to fighting in a manner halfway between the style of the LRDG and that of a regular force seeking to hold ground. Their spring 1942 campaign was thus a series of small raids and penetrations that lacked the depth and freedom of movement that characterized the activities of the LRDG. They also proved unable to successfully attack and hold any other Italian garrison of the size of Kufra and, when faced with organized Italian resistance, they were compelled to withdraw.

The strategic aims of the Free French were quite different from the British ones: the former sought to demonstrate that their army was still alive and kicking, the latter only sought to support the main battlefield farther north. Although Bagnold's development of LRDG doctrine was brilliant and innovative, it was also intrinsically linked to the geographical conditions of the Western Desert; once the Axis forces withdrew to the Tunisian beachhead, the role and effectiveness of the LRDG declined quickly. In Tunisia 'regular' special forces from both sides (British Commandos, US Rangers and German Brandenburgers) proved much more effective than they had been in the Western Desert, thanks both to an environment that more closely resembled Europe and the increased availability of men and resources. Although both the LRDG and the Italian Raggruppamento Sahariano fought in Tunisia, they did it in a more 'conventional' manner that bore little resemblance to the kind of war that had been waged in the deep desert. Eventually, the LRDG was transformed into a 'Commando-style' unit to fight in the Aegean islands. Bagnold's concepts and the deep desert raiding doctrine had apparently been short-lived, and soon fell into oblivion unlike other special forces units such as the SAS and Popski's Private Army, whose peculiarities enabled them to adjust to different terrain and missions. However, the basis behind Bagnold's doctrine survived intact: that there is no better special force than the one able to master enemy-held territory better than the enemy does.

Unit organization

British forces

The first British experience in modern desert warfare dates back to World War I, when General Archibald Murray's light armoured and motor machine-gun batteries in North Africa, and light car patrols in the Western Desert and Palestine allowed the assessment of many of the difficulties of operating in such an environment and also the beginning of the development of special equipment to overcome those difficulties. In the early 1920s, the need to bring Iraq's refractory Bedouin tribesmen under control ensured that British military attention remained focused on combat tactics in arid regions. In 1920–21, armoured cars manned by RAF personnel were employed to support the aerial campaign to crush the great Iraqi rebellion, which was a scheme partially developed by Colonel T. E. Lawrence. In the late 1920s and early 1930s further lessons were learned through the expeditions in the Western Desert led by the then Captain Ralph A. Bagnold, RSC, (later first CO of the LRDG), Guy L. Prendergast (later second CO of the LRDG), Patrick A. Clayton (later LRPU patrol commander) and William B. Kennedy-Shaw of the Sudan Colonial Service (later LRDG intelligence officer). At the outbreak of Word War II, the British Army therefore had a range of material dealing with the issues of operating small-scale units in the vast expanses between Egypt, Libya and Chad. The Long Range Patrol Units (LRPU, sometimes referred to as Long Range Desert Patrols – LRDP) were formed in July 1940 for long-range patrolling, scouting and raiding in the featureless 'sand sea' stretching westward from the Egyptian borders. Their creation had been proposed by the now Major Bagnold and was sanctioned by Lieutenant-General Sir Archibald Wavell – formerly a staff officer in General Allenby's Expeditionary Force and at the time Commander-in-Chief of the Middle East Command – with the aim of overcoming the operational limits of the British forces in North Africa. In Bagnold's opinion, these forces had 'only enough motor transport for a radius of action of a paltry 100 miles', and could cover just a very limited portion of Egypt's long desert border with

A well-loaded Chevrolet truck about to set off on patrol from Siwa. This vehicle was crewed by New Zealanders, many of whom joined the LRDG in 1940 from a consignment of troops who found themselves at Alexandria without their arms and equipment, which had been lost at sea. (IWM, E 012373)

Libya. They were therefore unable to cope with the developments in desert warfare made by the French and Italians: the former had been extending the activities of their *compagnies sahariennes* southward from the mid-1920s, whilst the latter started forming brand-new Auto-Saharan companies (*Compagnie Sahariane*) from 1923. From the outset mobility, autonomy and navigational skills were the key components of LRPU strategy. The LRPU had to be highly self-reliant, as each patrol needed to be able to operate as an independent force far from its supply bases in a largely unmapped and featureless region. Apart from the natural hardships of the desert, the main problems they had to face came from orientation, water and petrol consumption, and from communication shortcomings. Finally, vehicles had to be strong enough to endure mechanical fatigue, as well as to have sufficient firepower to deal with enemy convoys, their escorts and small desert outposts.

The LRDP began forming on 7 July 1940 under the command of Major Bagnold and drawing personnel from the New Zealand Division (mostly from the

divisional cavalry regiment, the 27th Machine-Gun Battalion, and the 7th Anti-Tank Regiment, RNZA). Lieutenant Kennedy-Shaw trained the first five navigators and, immediately after he joined the unit on 16 July, Captain Clayton began to organize the unit for operations. The original establishment of the LRDP comprised an HQ (CO, adjutant, quartermaster and intelligence officer plus 11 other ranks) and three four-troop patrols (labelled respectively: R Patrol, under Captain D. G. Steele; T Patrol, under Captain P. A. Clayton; and W Patrol, under Captain E. C. Mitford), plus signal, light repair and medical sections placed under the direct command of the HQ. Both T and W Patrols consisted of 25 men (a major or captain, a subaltern and 23 other ranks) and a dozen vehicles each, and both were intended as combat units while R Patrol was to act as a support unit. The patrols were initially split into A (22 men) and B (five men) Echelons. T, W and R Patrol's A echelons were each armed with ten Lewis machine guns, four Boys anti-tank rifles, and one Bofors anti-aircraft gun (or a 2in. mortar). There were also a great variety of individual weapons available, with a good number of automatic weapons to ensure adequate firepower. Communications were maintained with No. 11 wireless sets, while the vehicles were 30-cwt Chevrolet WB trucks, and 15-cwt Ford V8 trucks, either obtained from the Egyptian Army or bought in Cairo. The officers predominantly came from Bagnold's inner circle (as Prendergast, Clayton and Kennedy-Shaw did) and had a long experience in desert exploration. In August 1940, two (later four) six-wheeled Ford Marmon-Harrington trucks bought by an US oil-prospecting company were issued to R Patrol's B Echelon, which was subsequently renamed the Marmon-Harrington Party. R Patrol's A Echelon was subsequently reorganized as a combat patrol with the four customary troops (**Fig. 1**).

In September 1940 the Middle East Command asked the War Office for permission to double the strength of the LRDP, which was granted on the 29th. On 25 October a replacement scheme was approved and, finally, on 9 November 1940 the new scheme of organization of what was to be called the Long Range Desert Group was laid down. On paper it consisted of six patrols, each one composed of personnel drawn from a specific regiment: No. 1 Patrol from the Footguards, No. 2 from South Rhodesian units, No. 3 from the Highland

Three LRDG 30-cwt Chevrolet trucks, surrounded by desert. The 'desert scorpions' proved the most skilled masters of the environment during the North African campaign. (IWM, E 012385)

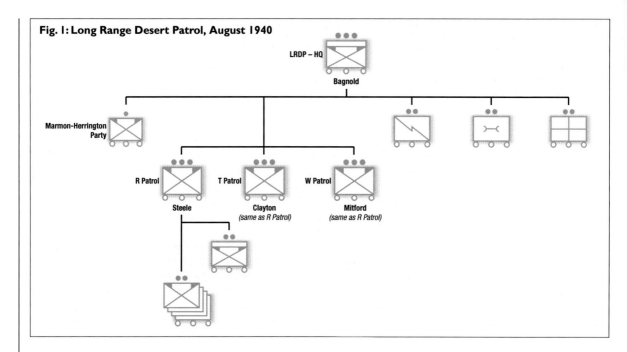

Fig. 1: Long Range Desert Patrol, August 1940

Table 1: Long Range Desert Patrol, August 1940

	Strength	Heavy weapons	Vehicles
Headquarters (signals section, light repair section, medical section)	4 officers (officer in command, quartermaster, intelligence, adjutant); 11 enlisted men		3 x Chewrolet WB 30-cwt, 4 x Ford V8 15-cwt
R Patrol (platoon HQ, four combat troops)	2 officers, 25 enlisted men	10 x Lewis MG, 4 x Boys AT rifles, 1 x Bofors 37mm gun (or 1 x 2in. mortar)	10 x Chevrolet WB 30-cwt, 1 x Ford V8 15-cwt
T Patrol	As above	As above	As above
W Patrol	As above	As above	As above
Marmon-Herrington Party (supply)	1 officer, 4 enlisted men		2 (later 4) x 6-ton Marmon-Herrington 6 x 6 lorries

Notes:
– LRDP began forming in July 1940
– R Patrol formed in August from A Echelon Supply Party, initially intended for supply purposes only
– Marmon-Herrington Party formed in August from the B Echelon Supply Party

regiments, No. 4 from the Yeomanry regiments, No. 5 from the Rifle regiments and No. 6 from the Home Counties regiments. Each patrol was to include a commander (captain), a subaltern, one sergeant, 31 other ranks and 37 Chevrolet trucks. However, neither the men nor the vehicles were available for such a reorganization. In late November 1940 the designation Long Range Desert Group (LRDG) was adopted while the structure was nominally expanded to two (later A and B) squadrons plus a heavy section (the Marmon-Herrington Party). The actual development was slower, and in early December W Patrol was disbanded and the New Zealanders returned to their units, while the vehicles and equipment were turned over to the newly formed G Patrol, which was formed from personnel of 3rd Battalion, Coldstream Guards, and the 2nd Battalion, Scots Guards, under Captain M. D. D. Chrichton-Stuart. No further reinforcements were available until early February 1941, though S Patrol began to assemble in

January 1941 from South Rhodesian (later South African) volunteers, additional personnel coming from the Northumberland Fusiliers and Argyll & Southerland Highlanders (**Fig. 2**). This reorganization also affected patrol organization, with each patrol split into two half patrols (Left and Right), each made of two troops: Right Half Patrol included HQ (green troop, also A Troop) and B Troop (black); Left Half Patrol included C and D Troops (yellow and red), each with three

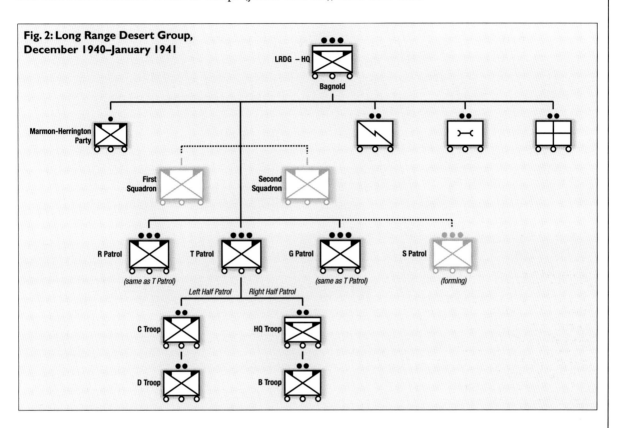

Fig. 2: Long Range Desert Group, December 1940–January 1941

LRDG – HQ
Bagnold

Marmon-Herrington Party

First Squadron

Second Squadron

R Patrol (same as T Patrol)

T Patrol

G Patrol (same as T Patrol)

S Patrol (forming)

Left Half Patrol | Right Half Patrol

C Troop

HQ Troop

D Troop

B Troop

Table 2: Long Range Desert Group, December 1940–January 1941

	Strength	Heavy weapons	Vehicles
Headquarters (signals section, light repair section, medical section)	7 officers, 6 NCOs, 56 enlisted men		3 x Chevrolet WB 30-cwt 4 x Ford V8 15-cwt
R Patrol (platoon HQ, three combat troops)	2 officers, 1 NCO, 27 enlisted men	HQ (A Tp): 1 x Vickers; B Tp: 3 x Lewis, 2 x Boys AT rifles; C Tp: 2 x Lewis, 1 x Bofors 37mm; D Tp: 3 x Lewis, 1 x Boys AT rifle	HQ (A Tp): 1 x Ford V8 15-cwt (crew 3) B – D Tps: each 3 x Chevrolet WB 30-cwt (each: crew 9)
T Patrol	As above	As above	As above
G Patrol	As above	As above	As above
S Patrol (forming)			12 x SPA AS37 trucks
Marmon-Herrington Party			4 x 6-ton Marmon-Herringtons

Notes:
– G Patrol formed in December 1940 (W Patrol disbanded the same month)
– S Patrol formed in January 1941
– Squadrons were intended but were not actually formed
– Breakdown into Right and Left Half Patrols was provisional

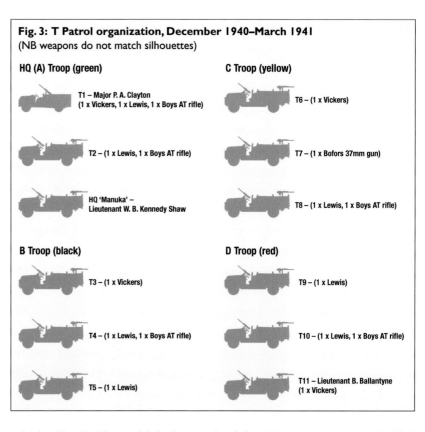

Fig. 3: T Patrol organization, December 1940–March 1941
(NB weapons do not match silhouettes)

HQ (A) Troop (green)

T1 – Major P. A. Clayton
(1 x Vickers, 1 x Lewis, 1 x Boys AT rifle)

T2 – (1 x Lewis, 1 x Boys AT rifle)

HQ 'Manuka' –
Lieutenant W. B. Kennedy Shaw

C Troop (yellow)

T6 – (1 x Vickers)

T7 – (1 x Bofors 37mm gun)

T8 – (1 x Lewis, 1 x Boys AT rifle)

B Troop (black)

T3 – (1 x Vickers)

T4 – (1 x Lewis, 1 x Boys AT rifle)

T5 – (1 x Lewis)

D Troop (red)

T9 – (1 x Lewis)

T10 – (1 x Lewis, 1 x Boys AT rifle)

T11 – Lieutenant B. Ballantyne
(1 x Vickers)

vehicles (**Fig. 3**). The established strength of the LRDG was more than doubled to around 300 men and 90 vehicles, with LRDG HQ (including signal, light repair and medical sections) rising to 69 men, and each patrol having 30 men and 12 vehicles. Their tasks became gradually more offensive, mixing traditional missions with raiding enemy strongpoints, airstrips, supply dumps and lines of communication.

Following the joint Franco-British raid into the Fezzan and the seizure of Kufra in April 1941, the LRDG transferred its main base from Abbassia Barracks in Cairo to Kufra itself. The creation of new patrols continued and, on 25 February 1941, Y Patrol was assembled under the command of Captain P. J. D. McCraith with personnel from the Nottinghamshire Yeomanry (Sherwood Rangers), part of 1st Cavalry Division in Palestine. Many of these new recruits proved unsuitable for the task in hand and the formation of Y Patrol was delayed until early March. Also in March an artillery section (H Section) was created, attached to B Squadron, equipped with a 25-pdr gun and a Vickers Mk VIb or Mk VIc light tank. H Section was disbanded between November and December 1941, as the weight of the equipment proved unsuitable for the LRDG's role. Following the formation of S Patrol and H Section, the LRDG was reorganized once more (**Fig. 4**), with the creation of a GHQ Squadron presiding over H Section and the Heavy Section, and the formation of two new squadrons: A Squadron, acting provisionally as a training squadron with G, S and Y Patrols, and B Squadron with T and R Patrols. On 7 June 1941, to cope with the increased activity of the LRDG, H Patrol

LRDG men cleaning their individual weapons before action. Even if the LRDG never proved suitable as a striking force, their firepower often inflicted significant losses on the enemy. (IWM, E 012438)

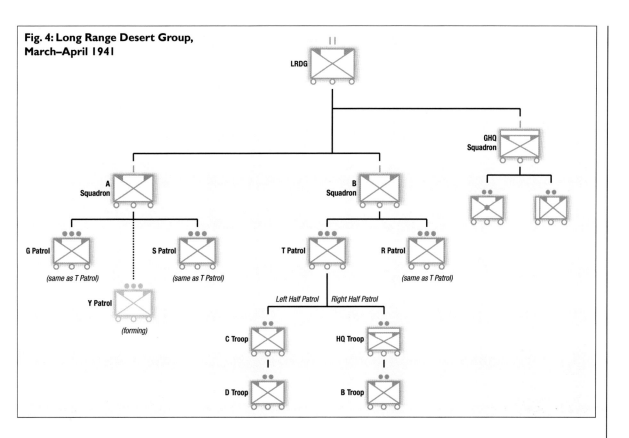

Fig. 4: Long Range Desert Group, March–April 1941

LRDG

GHQ Squadron

A Squadron

B Squadron

G Patrol *(same as T Patrol)*

S Patrol *(same as T Patrol)*

Y Patrol *(forming)*

T Patrol

R Patrol *(same as T Patrol)*

Left Half Patrol   Right Half Patrol

C Troop

HQ Troop

D Troop

B Troop

Table 3: Long Range Desert Group, March–April 1941

	Heavy weapons	Vehicles
Headquarters (heavy section, (RA) H Section)	1 x 25-pdr portéed, 1 x Vickers VI tank	30 x Ford F30 30-cwt, 4 x 10-ton White lorries, 2 x Mack NR4 lorries
Each patrol (platoon HQ, three combat troops)	HQ (A Tp): 1 x Vickers, 1 x Lewis, 1 x 2in. mortar; B Tp: 1 x Vickers, 2 x Lewis, 1 x Boys AT rifle; C Tp: 2 x Lewis, 1 x Bofors 37mm; D Tp: 1 x Vickers, 2 x Lewis, 1 x Boys AT rifle	HQ (A Tp): 1 x Ford V8; B – D Tps: each 3 x Chevrolet WB 30-cwt
Y Patrol		12 x SPA AS37 trucks

Notes:
– Y Patrol formed in February–March 1941
– H (Royal Artillery) and Heavy Sections (the latter from the Marmon-Herrington Party) formed March 1941; the former was attached to B Squadron
– Squadron HQs had an established strength of one officer, one warrant officer, one NCO and eight enlisted men
– Total strength of the LRDG was about 300 men and 90 vehicles

was formed from elements of G and Y Patrols (**Fig. 5**). The strength of A Squadron consisted of G, Y and H Patrols, each with six lorries divided between two troops. H Patrol was eventually disbanded in August–September 1941 and its personnel returned to their original units, leaving A Squadron with only two patrols until the reorganization of October 1941.

On 1 August 1941, Major Prendergast was promoted to the rank of lieutenant-colonel and assumed command of the LRDG, while Colonel Bagnold was transferred to the Eighth Army HQ (Eighth Army was actually formed on 24 September). Also, by mid-July the LRDG had been relieved of its defensive duties at Kufra, and the time came for further reorganization. In early August G and Y Patrols were sent back to Cairo for rest and refitting, followed by the end of the month by HQ (A) Squadron, which was renamed B Squadron, and T Patrol. A new A Squadron was formed at Siwa consisting of R and S Patrols plus Group HQ and the Heavy Section. From October 1941 the role of the LRDG evolved from long-range reconnaissance and intelligence gathering to include more 'hit and run' operations to support the coming offensive in November 1941 (Operation *Crusader*). Men from the disbanded Layforce (Nos. 7, 8, and 11 Commandos, transferred to Egypt in March 1941, plus the locally raised Combined Middle East Commando) joined the ranks, with the aim of increasing the LRDG's sabotage potential. The light repair and signal sections were set up as distinct units with their own establishments, and both were placed under the direct command of LRDG's HQ, which also presided over a newly formed survey and air sections, the latter equipped with two Waco biplanes. At the same time the patrol structure of the LRDG was reorganized to both increase mobility and reduce the risk of detection. The patrols were split into half patrols (numbered 1 and 2), with four 30-cwt Ford F30 lorries and one 15-cwt Chevrolet lorry going to the first half patrol, and six 30-cwt Ford F30 lorries going to the second half patrol. Squadron HQs were also equipped with two 15-cwt Chevrolet lorries, one of them fitted with a 2in. mortar (**Fig. 6**). On

Table 4: Long Range Desert Group, June 1941		
	Heavy weapons	**Vehicles**
G, Y, H Patrols	2 x Vickers, 4 x Lewis, I x Boys or I x .50-cal. Vickers HMG or I x 37mm Bofors	6 x Ford F30, I x Ford V8
R, S, T Patrols (platoon HQ, three combat troops)	HQ (A Tp): I x Vickers, I x Lewis, I x 2in. mortar; B Tp: I x Vickers, 2 x Lewis, I x Boys AT rifle; C Tp: 2 x Lewis, I x Bofors 37mm; D Tp: I x Vickers, 2 x Lewis, I x Boys AT rifle	HQ (A Tp): I x Ford V8, I x Ford F30 Signal truck; B–D Tps: each 3 x Chevrolet WB 30-cwt

Notes:
– H Patrol formed in June 1941 from elements of G and Y Patrols; subsequently disbanded in August/September
– G, Y and H Patrols were half patrols at that time

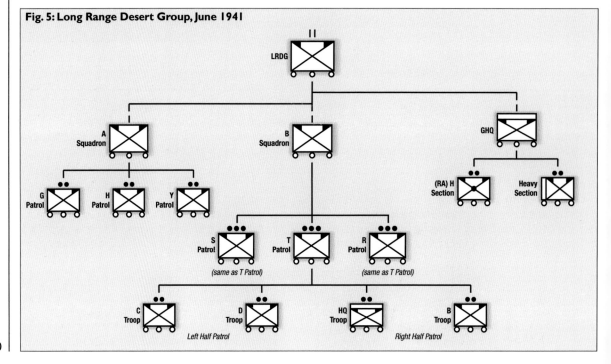

Fig. 5: Long Range Desert Group, June 1941

1 October 1941 the LRDG was subordinated to Lt. Gen. Cunningham's Eighth Army and, by the end of the month, both A and B Squadrons, with all their attached half patrols, were fully operational based at Siwa.

Operation *Crusader* put this new establishment under a heavy strain. The main tasks of the LRDG were observation of the movement in the areas of Bir Hacheim, El Adem, Mekili, Bir Tengeder, Giof el Etel and along the northern approaches to the Jalo Oasis. They were also to cooperate with both Force E, led

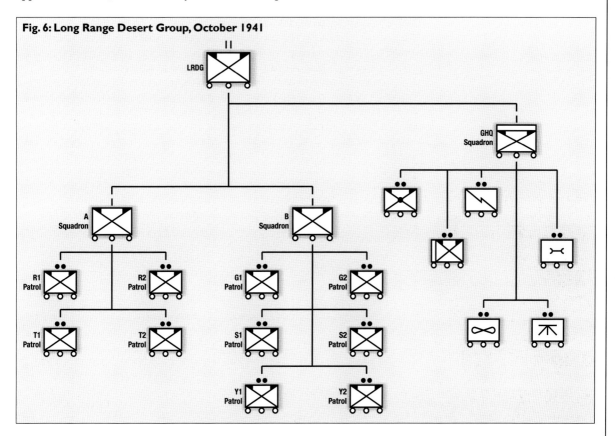

Fig. 6: Long Range Desert Group, October 1941

Table 5: Long Range Desert Group, October 1941		
	Heavy weapons	**Vehicles**
GHQ ((RA) H Section, heavy section, light repair section, signals section, air section, survey section)	I x Vicker VI tank, I x 25-pdr	I x 4 x 2 ambulance, 2 x Ford F8 signals, 2 x Mack NR4 6 x 6 lorries, 4 x 10-ton White lorries, I x Fiat SPA workshop truck, I x Fiat SPA radio van, 2 x Waco biplanes, 3 x Ford F30 lorries
A Squadron (R1, R2, T1, T2 Patrols)	Sqdn HQ: I x 2in. mortar; First half patrols: 2 x Vickers, 3 x Lewis, I x Boys AT rifle; Second half patrols: I x 37mm Bofors, 4 x Lewis, I x Vickers, I x Boys AT rifle	Sqdn HQ: 2 x Chevrolet 15-cwt; First half patrols: I x Chevrolet 15-cwt, 4 x Ford F30; Second half patrols: 6 x Ford F30
B Squadron (G1, G2, S1, S2, Y1, Y2 Patrols)	As above	As above

Notes:
– Reorganization took place in October; by the end of the month patrols were back to their duty. The (RA) H Section was subsequently disbanded in November/December 1941, while in January/February 1942 the light repair section became a light repair squadron with an HQ and two troops.

by Brigadier D. W. Reid, and the newly formed Special Air Service (SAS), led by Captain David Stirling. Stirling's SAS had been created in July 1941 from Layforce personnel to serve as a parachute detachment to raid enemy lines of communication and by summer 1942 it had a strength of about 100. Renamed L Detachment, Special Air Service, it proved to unable to carry out its original task: in fact, the only airborne mission it ever carried out, on the night of 16/17 November 1941, ended in failure and the loss of 32 out of 53 men. The men of the SAS were specialized in sabotage and supplied a complementary force to the LRDG, whose skills did not include those particular forms of warfare. The LRDG carried SAS parties close to their objectives and took them back to base following the completion of their missions; the SAS parties performed the sabotage missions that the LRDG was not suited to carrying out.

Operation *Crusader* saw LRDG patrols scattered over a wide area and frequently detached to other units. In particular, between 17 and 26 November 1941, R1 Patrol was tasked to recover the SAS men that had been dropped to raid the enemy airstrips at Tmimi and in the Gazala area. The mission ended in failure, though it proved a useful experience for further LRDG/SAS joint operations. In fact, less than a month later (on 8 December), S1 Patrol and an SAS party led by Captain Stirling performed the first joint mission raiding the airstrip at Sirte; the mission was highly successful, and served as a template for later operations. In late December 1941, all the patrols detached to other units finally returned under LRDG control, although cooperation with the SAS and other strike forces continued. In early January 1942, a few days before Rommel launched his counteroffensive, LRDG's HQ was transferred to Jalo, though some days later, under German pressure, it redeployed first in Maaten Ghetmir (some 20 miles from Jalo) and then, on 1 February 1942, to Siwa. Losses caused some patrols to withdraw to Cairo for rest and refit, though B Squadron (with four patrols attached and one, R2, with Free French forces) remained at Siwa.

This period saw a further reorganization of the force, with an expanded LRDG HQ, consisting of the heavy, air, survey, light repair and signal sections, to which was also attached an HQ squadron (A Squadron) consisting of six patrols (R1, R2, S1, S2, T1 and T2); there was also a detachable squadron (B Squadron) of four

Y Patrol resting in front of one of their trucks at Air Ghetmir. David Lloyd Owen, the patrol commander, is standing on the extreme left. The truck in the background is a four-wheel drive Ford F30. These trucks didn't prove satisfactory and, by March 1942, were all replaced by the Chevrolet 30-cwt. (IWM, HU 016454)

patrols (G1, G2, Y1 and Y2). The actual subordination of patrols to squadron often varied depending upon the needs of each individual mission. A sabotage platoon was suposed to be attached to B Squadron, but this was never created. Chevrolet 30-cwt trucks were reintroduced to replace the more oil-thirsty Ford F30s that had reached the end of their operative life, and four 10-ton Macks trucks replaced the worn-out White trucks of the heavy section. The firepower of individual patrols was also increased as a reflection of the Axis forces increasingly aggressive posture (**Fig. 7**).

In spring 1942, the LRDG was widely employed both on reconnaissance and for guiding or collecting sabotage parties. According to an Eighth Army instruction of 9 March 1942, 'every effort' had to be made 'to weaken the enemy main forces, to cause him to disperse his efforts, and, in particular, to lower his morale', by carrying out 'intensive sabotage' against airstrips, lines of communication, bases, supply dumps and repair facilities. This new period of LRDG activity was marked by a series of LRDG and SAS joint actions that included raids on Barce and Benina airstrips, Bengazi harbour and the Slonta area. This increased role brought about a correspondent increase in the strength of the unit. In April 1942 A and C Squadrons from the Middle East Commando were attached. In May, J (Jats) and R (Rajput) Patrols were attached from the Long Range Desert Squadron IAC (also known as the Indian Long Range Squadron – ILRS). This had been formed on 25 December 1941 based on volunteers from the 2nd Royal Lancers, Prince Albert Victor's Own Cavalry (11th Frontier Force) and 18th King Edward VII's Own Cavalry. After they joined the LRDG, the Indian patrols were relabelled as I1 and I2. During this period the LRDG's actual establishment included only one squadron (A Squadron), to which all the patrols were subordinated (**Fig. 8**). At the end of

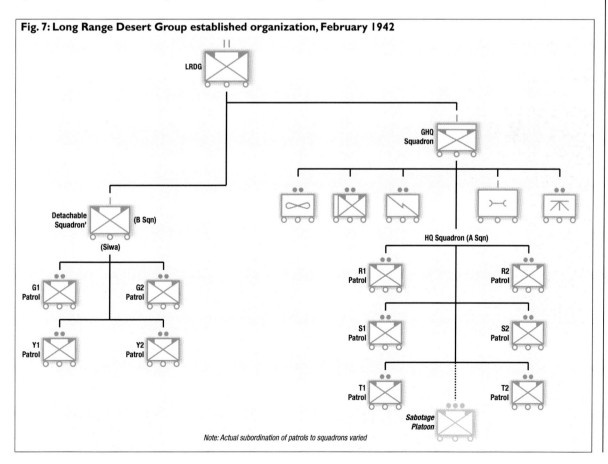

Fig. 7: Long Range Desert Group established organization, February 1942

Note: Actual subordination of patrols to squadrons varied

Table 6: Long Range Desert Group established organization, February 1942

	Personnel	Heavy weapons	Vehicles
LRDG Squadron HQ (heavy section, light repair squadron, survey section, signals section, air section	8 officers, 7 WO/NCOs, 40 enlisted men (11 attached – 1 x medical officer, 10 enlisted men)		1 x motorcycle, 1 x 4-seater car, 7 x Chevrolet 15-cwt, 7 x Chevrolet 30-cwt, 6 x 3-tonlorries, 6 x 10-ton lorries, 2 Waco biplanes
3 patrols, each:	1 officers, 1 WO/NCO, 13 enlisted men	2 x Vickers .50-cal., 3 x Vickers .303in. K, 1 x Vickers .303in., 5 x Lewis, 1 x 20mm Breda	6 x Chevrolet 30-cwt
3 patrols, each:	1 officer, 14 enlisted men	2 x Vickers .50-cal., 3 x Vickers .303in. K, 1 x Vickers .303in., 5 x Lewis, 1 x 20mm Breda	6 x Chevrolet 30-cwt
Sabotage Platoon (formation proposed but not carried out)	4 officers, 1 WO/NCO, 19 enlisted men		
Detachable Squadron HQ	1 officer, 2 WO/NCOs, 8 enlisted men		1 x Chevrolet 15-cwt, 5 x Chevrolet 30-cwt
2 patrols, each:	1 officer, 1 WO/NCO, 13 enlisted men	2 x Vickers .50-cal., 3 x Vickers .303in. K, 1 x Vickers .303in., 5 x Lewis, 1 x 20mm Breda	6 x Chevrolet 30-cwt
2 patrols, each:	1 officers 14 enlisted men	2 x Vickers .50-cal., 3 x Vickers .303in. K, 1 x Vickers .303in., 5 x Lewis, 1 x 20mm Breda	6 x Chevrolet 30-cwt

Weapons: 66 pistols, 180 .303in. rifles, 30 carbines, 93 LMGs, 13 Vickers .303in. MG, 26 Vickers .5in. MG, 12 20mm Breda, 3 3in. mortars

June 1942, following Rommel's new offensive, LRDG's HQ left Siwa, A and C Squadrons, MEC, were definitively detached, while A Squadron's HQ moved to Kufra to cooperate with the SAS. Following the 'big raids' of September 1942, and in view of the future counteroffensive, a new reorganization took place, which this time included the SAS. L Detachment now became the 1st Special Air Service Regiment, composed of a regimental HQ and an HQ squadron that included administration and depot, intelligence, signals and parachute training troops, and a light repair squadron. L Detachment was now composed of two squadrons (A and B), each with three troops made up of two operational sections and a personnel and supply section. A new M Detachment was raised consisting of C and D Squadrons, and a Free French Squadron was attached (as, later, was the Greek 'Sacred' Squadron). The Folboat Section, originating from the Special Boat Section, was also attached (**Fig. 9**).

On 1 October 1942, the remnant of the ILRS (HQ plus M – Muslim – and S – Sikh – Patrols) was transferred to the LRDG, and incorporated as I3 and I4 Patrols. Thus, before the Alamein offensive, the LRDG reached its peak strength, further increased by the addition on 10 December of 'Popski's Private Army' (PPA) as No. 1 Special Demolition Squad (**Fig. 10**). On 28 December 1942 the LRDG HQ moved to Zella and, on 16 January 1943, to Hon. After a brief involvement in Tunisia from the last week of March to the first week of April 1943, all LRDG units finally returned to Egypt, soon followed by ILRS ones, thus officially closing their North African campaign.

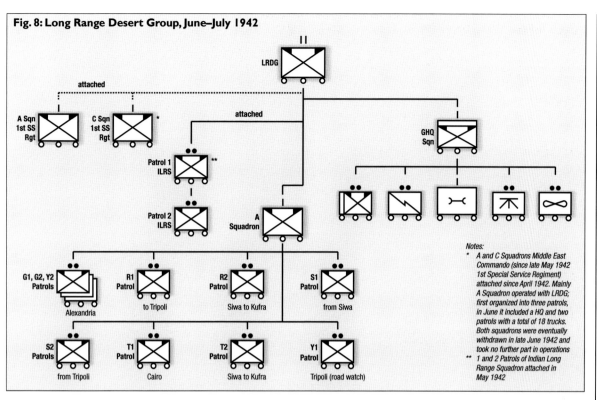

Fig. 8: Long Range Desert Group, June–July 1942

Notes:
* A and C Squadrons Middle East Commando (since late May 1942 1st Special Service Regiment) attached since April 1942. Mainly A Squadron operated with LRDG; first organized into three patrols, in June it included a HQ and two patrols with a total of 18 trucks. Both squadrons were eventually withdrawn in late June 1942 and took no further part in operations
** 1 and 2 Patrols of Indian Long Range Squadron attached in May 1942

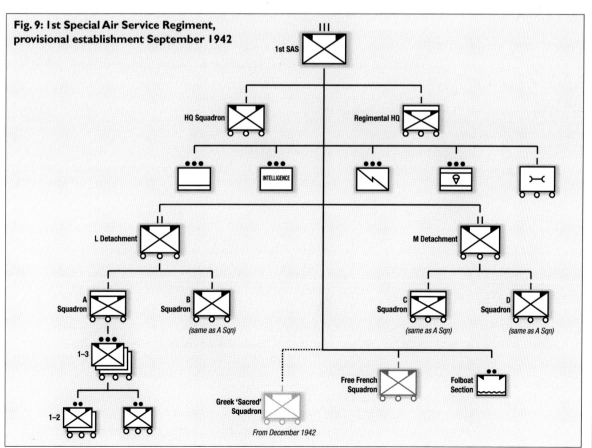

Fig. 9: 1st Special Air Service Regiment, provisional establishment September 1942

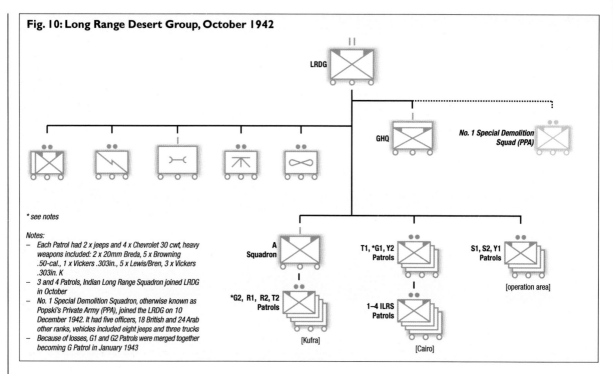

Fig. 10: Long Range Desert Group, October 1942

LRDG

GHQ

No. 1 Special Demolition Squad (PPA)

A Squadron

T1, *G1, Y2 Patrols

S1, S2, Y1 Patrols

*G2, R1, R2, T2 Patrols

1–4 ILRS Patrols

[operation area]

[Kufra]

[Cairo]

* see notes

Notes:
– Each Patrol had 2 x jeeps and 4 x Chevrolet 30 cwt, heavy weapons included: 2 x 20mm Breda, 5 x Browning .50-cal., 1 x Vickers .303in., 5 x Lewis/Bren, 3 x Vickers .303in. K
– 3 and 4 Patrols, Indian Long Range Squadron joined LRDG in October
– No. 1 Special Demolition Squadron, otherwise known as Popski's Private Army (PPA), joined the LRDG on 10 December 1942. It had five officers, 18 British and 24 Arab other ranks, vehicles included eight jeeps and three trucks
– Because of losses, G1 and G2 Patrols were merged together becoming G Patrol in January 1943

Italian forces

At the outbreak of war in North Africa, the Italian Army in Libya was still largely a colonial force. Native Libyan forces included two divisions, seven fusilier battalions, four cavalry groups, two blackshirt groups, one parachute battalion and more than 40 assorted companies. In August 1940, 22,000 out of the 189,000 soldiers in North Africa were Libyan, and 3,632 of them (along with 149 officers

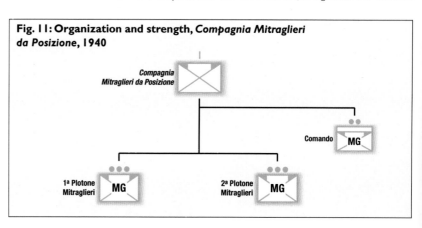

Fig. 11: Organization and strength, *Compagnia Mitraglieri da Posizione*, 1940

Compagnia Mitraglieri da Posizione

Comando MG

1ª Plotone Mitraglieri MG

2ª Plotone Mitraglieri MG

Table 7: Organization and strength, *Compagnia Mitraglieri da Posizione* 1940

	Officers	NCOs	Enlisted men, Italian	Enlisted men, Libyan	Pistols	Rifles	MGs
Comando	1	1	3	10	2	14	1
Plotone mitraglieri (x 2)	1	0	0	50	13	38	6*
Total	3	1	3	110	28	90	13

* two squads each with 3 MGs

and 952 Italian other ranks) were stationed in the Libyan Sahara. These units included garrison troops like the 11ª Compagnie Mitraglieri da Posizione (fixed machine-gun company), camel-mounted units like the 4ª Compagnie Meharisti and the Gruppo Cammellato Tuareg, but also included five of the renowned *Compagnie Sahariane*. First formed in 1923, their most notable achievement was the conquest of the Kufra Oasis in January 1931. In 1938, four years after his appointment as governor-general of Libya, Marshal Italo Balbo motorized and reorganized the *Compagnie Sahariane* into a single unit, which also included a light aircraft section.

Garrisoning the Sahara was a mixture of units of different kind and quality: the *Compagnie Mitraglieri da Posizione* (**Fig. 11**) were weak but heavily armed units designed only for garrison duties. The *Compagnie Meharisti* (**Fig. 12**) were stronger in terms of manpower, but had less firepower. The *Compagnie Sahariane* (**Fig. 13**) were equivalent to the *Compagnie Mitraglieri* in terms of manpower but had better firepower and were manoeuvrable, which placed them amongst the best Libyan units available.

At the outbreak of the war, the defence of the Libyan Sahara was in the hands of the Comando Fronte Sud (Southern Front Command). Most of its troops were deployed on the western border, close to the French-held colonies, and at Kufra. In July 1940, soon after the fall of France, the three-company

A group of Italian soldiers waits for orders lined up inside a fort in the Sahara. Following the successful LRDG and Free French raids in the Fezzan during the winter of 1940/41, several company-strength Italian Army units were deployed in the area to strengthen the local defences. It is interesting to note that Italian soldiers seem to have been the only ones to have used the tropical helmet throughout the war in the desert. Their uniform was similar to the one worn in Europe, though made of lightweight fabric. (Piero Crociani)

A group of *Meharisti del Fezzan*, the Libyan camel-mounted troops (their name derived from the Arab term *Mehara*, camel). Though obsolete, *Meharisti* units were still used in 1940 and even up till late 1942. The camel, unlike the horse, was not suitable for combat due to its height and speed, and the *Meharisti* always fought dismounted. The flag sported by the man in the foreground bears their insignia. (Piero Crociani)

Table 8: Organization and strength, *Compagnia Meharisti* 1940

	Officers	NCOs	Enlisted men, Italian	Enlisted men, Libyan	Camels	Pistols	Rifles	LMG
Comando	4	1	0	17	49	2	22	1
Plotone Meharisti (x 4)	1	1	1	71	85	6	71	3
Total	8	5	4	301	389	26	306	13

Note:
– On 29 December 1940 the 4ª Plotone was equipped with six HMGs and transformed into a Plotone Mitraglieri (the company had now 12 LMGs and six HMGs)

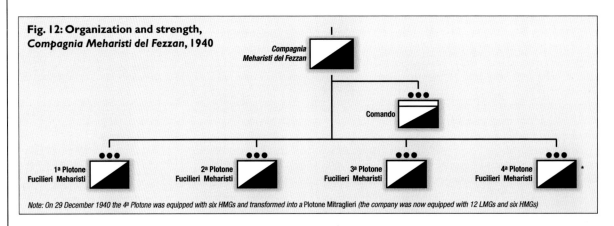

Fig. 12: Organization and strength, *Compagnia Meharisti del Fezzan*, 1940

Compagnia Meharisti del Fezzan

Comando

1ª Plotone Fucilieri Meharisti

2ª Plotone Fucilieri Meharisti

3ª Plotone Fucilieri Meharisti

4ª Plotone Fucilieri Meharisti

Note: On 29 December 1940 the 4ª Plotone was equipped with six HMGs and transformed into a Plotone Mitraglieri (the company was now equipped with 12 LMGs and six HMGs)

Battaglione Sahariano was activated (a fourth followed in December), which became part of the Raggruppamento Maletti (Battlegroup Maletti) that advanced to Sidi Barrani in September, where it was eventually destroyed in January 1941 during Operation *Compass*. By December 1940, when the threat from the LRDG and Free French forces was beginning to materialize, the Comando del Sahara Libico (Libyan Sahara Command, Comando Fronte Sud's new designation from mid-August 1940) had already been depleted of its best troops (**Fig. 14**), a condition further worsened by the loss of the two *Compagnie Mitraglieri* (59ª and 60ª) and a *Compagnia Sahariana* at Kufra in March 1941.

On 25 February 1941, even before the loss of Kufra and Jarabub, O'Connor's advance into Cyrenaica provoked a major reorganization and strengthening of the Saharan forces. The emphasis of the defence was shifted towards the south and east, while Italian Army anti-tank and artillery units joined local

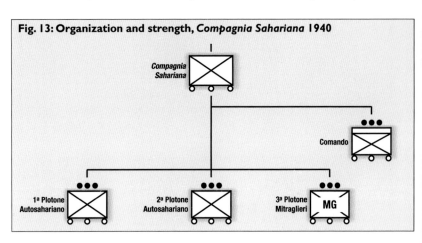

Fig. 13: Organization and strength, *Compagnia Sahariana* 1940

Compagnia Sahariana

Comando

1ª Plotone Autosahariano

2ª Plotone Autosahariano

3ª Plotone Mitraglieri — MG

Table 9: Organization and strength, *Compagnia Sahariana* 1940

	Officers	NCOs	Enlisted men, Italian	Enlisted men, Libyan	Pistols	Rifles	LMGs	HMGs	AS 37	Lorries
Comando	I	4	17	5	5	26	0	0	4*	3
Plotone Autosahariano (x 2)	I	I	5	25	5	28	3	0	4	0
Plotone Mitraglieri	I	I	5	22	10	20	0	4	4	0
Total	4	7	32	77	25	112	6	4	16	3

* one of which was equipped with a radio

Note:
– At the disposal of the five Compagnie Sahariane were two Sezioni Aeroplani, each equipped with four reconnaissance and liaison planes. At least four were twin-engined Caproni Ghibli. The established strength of each section (belonging to the Regia Aeronautica) was:

Officers	NCOs	Enlisted men	Pistols	Rifles	Fiat 634/N
4	4	32	4	36	24

Fig. 14: Comando del Sahara Libico, December 1940

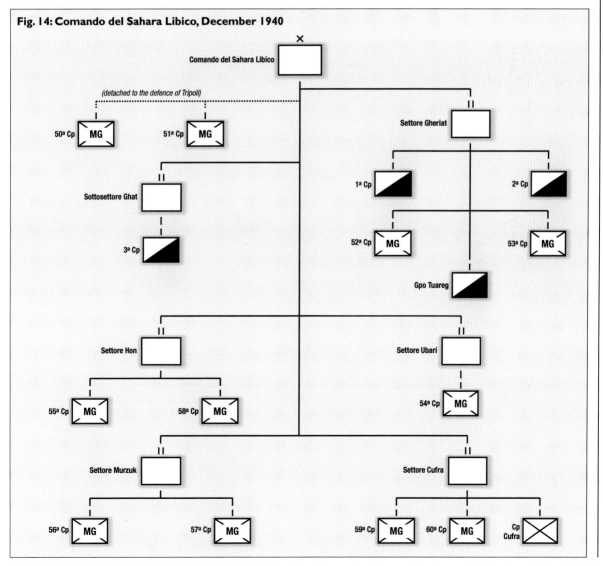

garrisons, new weapons became available and five 'mobile columns' were set up. The situation improved dramatically after 3 March 1941, when General Umberto Piatti Dal Pozzo took over command of the Comando del Sahara Libico. On 15 March 1941 he formed five new *Compagnie Sahariane* from the mobile columns, and reorganized and strengthened the defences both at Hon (where the 61ª Compagnia Mitraglieri was formed on 16 March) and in the Murzuk area (**Fig. 15**).

However, there still were many difficulties: supply issues caused some units to move northwards; Rommel's advance into Cyrenaica took other units – including the 1ª Compagnia Sahariana – away from the Sahara; and, finally, growing concerns about the reliability of the Libyan troops meant that only those units that were 'indispensable and reliable' were maintained.

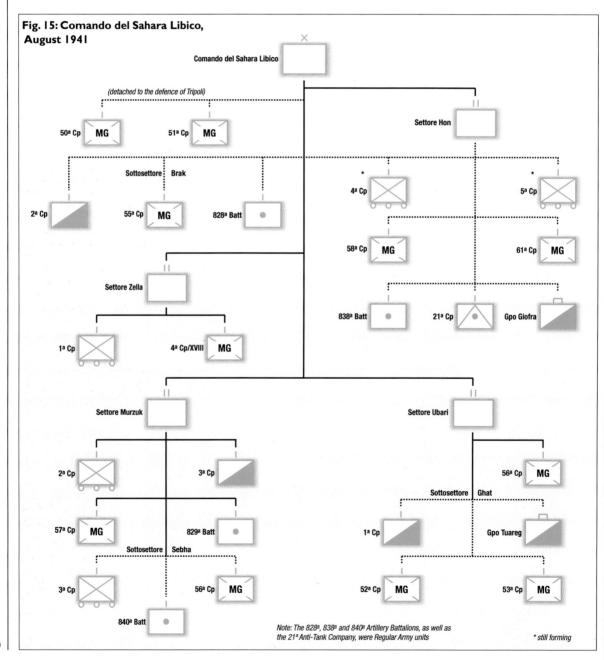

Fig. 15: Comando del Sahara Libico, August 1941

Note: The 828ª, 838ª and 840ª Artillery Battalions, as well as the 21ª Anti-Tank Company, were Regular Army units

* still forming

30

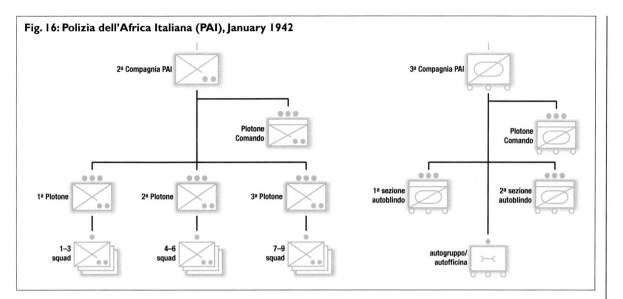

Fig. 16: Polizia dell'Africa Italiana (PAI), January 1942

All these factors affected the actual strength of the Comando Sahara Libico; after a temporary contraction (in October 1940 it included 121 Italian officers and 594 other ranks, plus 2,866 Libyan soldiers) by February 1941 its numbers matched those of the previous August with 149 officers, 225 NCOs, 735 Italian soldiers and 3,696 Libyan soldiers. These figures remained substantially unchanged until September and eventually dropped in October 1941, when the Comando Sahara Libico contained 130 officers, 174 NCOs, 780 Italian soldiers and 2,991 Libyan soldiers. The heavy weapons available included 28 Breda 20mm guns, 16 AT 47/32 guns and 16 77/28 guns; there were also 144 serviceable and 113 unserviceable vehicles.

However, the effectiveness of the Italian forces was patchy: most of the *Compagnie Mitraglieri* were still considered unreliable, while only the *Compagnie Sahariane* and the *Compagnie Meharisti* were considered effective combat units. The latter were only partly effective as they lacked motor vehicles and were still

Three Libyan soldiers showing a mixture of uniforms and insignia. On the right and left are Libyan *Carabinieri*, or *Zaptié* (a term derived from the Turkish word *zaptiye*, meaning police officer), both wearing the characteristic *tachia* (turban) with the khaki cover. The one in the middle is an infantry soldier wearing a fez and carrying a cloth band rolled up around his waist in the colours of the corps to which he belonged. (Piero Crociani)

A Libyan mortar team manning an 81mm mortar in what looks like a practice drill. Until spring 1942 the Libyan units were only armed with light weapons and machine guns; from this point they began to be issued with mortars and anti-tank guns to improve their firepower. (Piero Crociani)

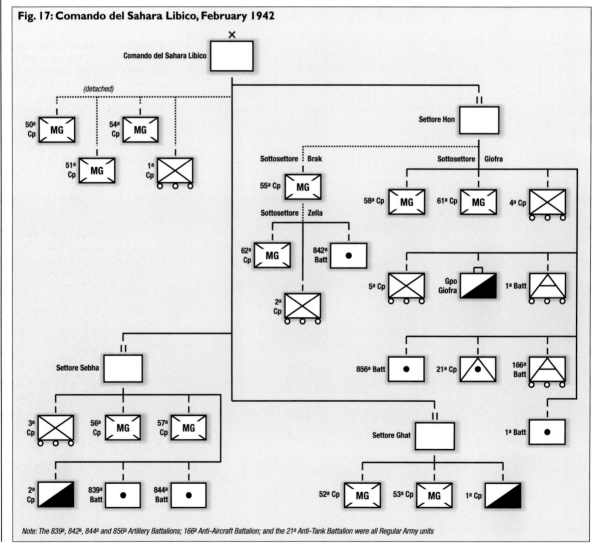

Fig. 17: Comando del Sahara Libico, February 1942

Note: The 839ᵃ, 842ᵃ, 844ᵃ and 856ᵃ Artillery Battalions; 166ᵃ Anti-Aircraft Battalion; and the 21ᵃ Anti-Tank Battalion were all Regular Army units

forced to use camels, which, by late 1941, was a serious shortcoming. General Piatti Dal Pozzo, commanding officer of the Comando Saharo Libica, realized that only motorized units could be effective against the LRDG and the Free French forces, and reacted accordingly, creating a a new 'mobile column' on 8 November 1941 from the 21ª Compagnia Cannoni and the 5ª Compagnia Sahariana. This fully motorized column comprised an anti-tank section (four 47/32 guns), an AA section (four 20mm Breda) and an infantry section with seven AS 37 light trucks. Although it was eventually disbanded in mid-March 1942, the column proved that only motorized units could effectively patrol the desert.

In spite of their numerous mistakes, the Italians did finally acknowledge the value of motorized units, though the lack of trained personnel and suitable vehicles delayed the development of Italian desert raiding forces. By January 1942 the strength of the Comando Sahara Libico had not grown considerably from the previous October: there were 130 Italian officers, 204 NCOs and 796 other ranks, plus 2,869 Libyan colonial troops. Heavy weapons still included 28 20mm AA guns, 16 47/32 AT guns and 16 77/28 AT guns, plus eight more 37/54 AT guns and three 75/27 guns. There were 155 serviceable and 90 unserviceable vehicles (**Fig. 17**). Only after the Free French raids in the Fezzan region were Italian forces in the Sahara reorganized and motorized raiding parties set up. On 25 March 1942 (five days after the formation of the 6ª Compagnia Sahariana) the war establishments of both the *Compagnie Libice* – as the *Compagnie Mitraglieri* were renamed – and the *Compagnie Sahariane* were revised (**Figs. 18** and **19**), with a more flexible formula ntroduced that sacrificed manpower for firepower. In March 1942, Piatti Dal Pozzo further strengthened his front line by transferring most of the available units to the Sebha sector, which affected the ratio of Libyan to Italian troops in the area. By 1 November

A sentry keeps watch from an observation post on top of a fort somewhere in the desert. The presence of a number of garrisons spread throughout the desert was a characteristic feature of Italian defensive organization in North Africa; this arrangement was designed to subdue the hostile local population. (Piero Crociani)

An Italian officer rides a camel in the Arab style. He wears the white uniform that was authorized for use by troops serving in the lowland regions of Italian East Africa and the Sahara. (Piero Crociani)

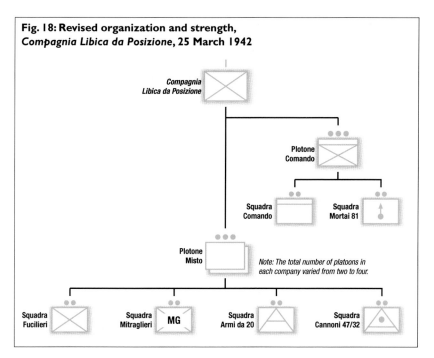

Fig. 18: Revised organization and strength,
Compagnia Libica da Posizione, 25 March 1942

Compagnia Libica da Posizione

Plotone Comando

Squadra Comando

Squadra Mortai 81

Plotone Misto

Note: The total number of platoons in each company varied from two to four.

Squadra Fucilieri

Squadra Mitraglieri — MG

Squadra Armi da 20

Squadra Cannoni 47/32

Table 10: Revised organization and strength, *Compagnia Libica da Posizione*, 25 March 1942

	Officers	NCOs	Enlisted men, Italian	Enlisted men, Libyan
Plotone Comando	1	2	2	22
Plotone Misto	1	-	-	36

Note:
– The number of mixed platoons (plotone misto) varied between each company. The Squadra Mortai da 81 (81mm mortar squad) had two mortars, the Squadra Armi da 20 (20mm weapons squad) had either 20mm cannons or anti-tank rifles, the Squadra Cannoni da 47/32 (47/32 anti-tank gun squad) had a single 47/32 piece

Fig. 19: Revised organization and strength, *Compagnia Sahariana*, 25 March 1942

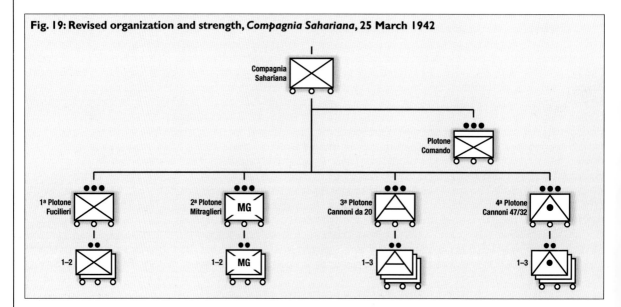

Comando Sahara Libico's strength included 251 officers, 334 NCOs and 2,502 Italian other ranks, compared to 2,721 Libyan soldiers. Heavy weapons also increased accordingly: apart from 28 light tanks and ten armoured cars, the Comando had 72 AT guns, 83 20mm Breda AA guns and 50 other guns. There were also 225 serviceable and 157 unserviceable vehicles (**Fig. 20**).

Three factors affected this decisive switch in Italian strategy in the Sahara: firstly, the influence of the German Sonderkommando Dora; secondly, the Axis advance into Egypt opened new horizons; finally, the availability of a large amount of British booty provided the Italians with a large number of desert-going vehicles. In late May 1942 Piatti Dal Pozzo proposed the formation of small raiding parties with the aim of harassing the Allied land and air communications

A PAI motorcycl team somewhere along the Via Balbia in early 1942. From January 1942 the 2ª Compagnia of the PAI Battalion 'Romolo Gessi' was employed on road security duties along the main roads in Cyrenaica along with the Italian military police, the *Carabinieri*, and the German *Feldgendarmerie*. (Piero Crociani)

Table 11: Revised organization and strength, *Compagnia Sahariana*, 25 March 1942

	Officers	NCOs	Enlisted men, Italian	Enlisted men, Libyan	LMGs	HMGs	Lorries
Plotone Comando	1	3	2	18	0	0	3 autocarri AS; 2 camion Lancia RO
Plotone Fucilieri	1	0	0	31	2	0	4 autocarri AS
Plotone Mitraglieri	1	0	0	31	0	2	2 camion Lancia RO
Plotone Cannoni da 20	1	0	0	25	0	0	3 camion Lancia RO each with a 20mm gun
Plotone Cannoni da 47/32	1	0	0	28	0	0	3 camion Lancia RO each with a 47/32 gun
Total	5	3	2	133	2	2	7 autocarri AS 10 camion Lancia RO

Note:
– Each company had to carry enough water for ten days, food for 15 days and fuel for 1,000km

Fig. 20: Comando del Sahara Libico, October 1942

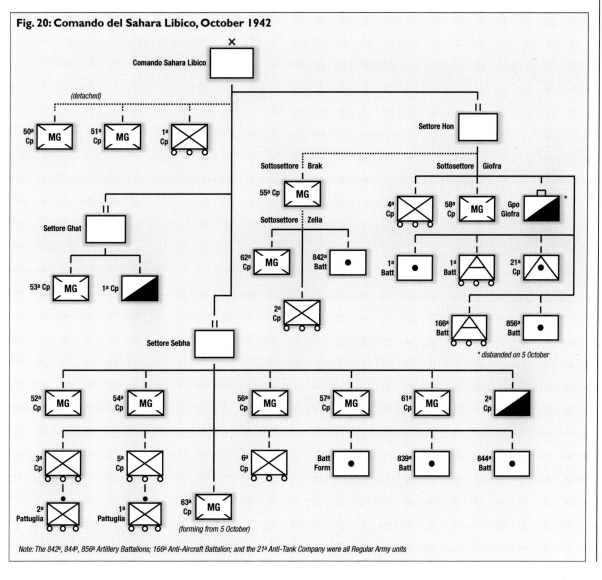

Note: The 842ª, 844ª, 856ª Artillery Battalions; 166ª Anti-Aircraft Battalion; and the 21ª Anti-Tank Company were all Regular Army units

Table 12: Comando Sahara del Libico, October 1942

Comando Sahara del Libico

Detached to other commands:

    50ª Compagnia Libica da Posizione

    51ª Compagnia Libica da Posizione

    1ª Compagnia Sahariana

Settore Hon (defence sector Hon)

    Sottosettore Giofra (sub-sector Giofra)

        4ª Compagnia Sahariana

        58ª Compagnia Libica da Posizione

        Gruppo Bande Giofra

        1ª Batteria Sahariana da 75/27

        1ª Batteria Sahariana da 20mm

        21ª Compagnia Cannoni da 47/32

        166ª Batteria da 20mm

        856ª Batteria da 77/28

    Sottosettore Brak (sub-sector Brak)

        55ª Compagnia Libica da Posizione

    Sottosettore Zella (sub-sector Zella)

        2ª Compagnia Sahariana

        62ª Compagnia Libica da Posizione

        842ª Batteria da 77/28

Settore Ghat (defence sector Ghat)

    53ª Compagnia Libica da Posizione

    1ª Compagnia Meharisti

Settore Sebha (defence sector Sebha)

    52ª Compagnia Libica da Posizione

    54ª Compagnia Libica da Posizione

    56ª Compagnia Libica da Posizione

    57ª Compagnia Libica da Posizione

    61ª Compagnia Libica da Posizione

    63ª Compagnia Libica da Posizione (airfield garrison, forming from 5 October 1942)

    2ª Compagnia Meharisti

    3ª Compagnia Sahariana, with:

    19ª squadra di pilotaggio zone desertiche

    pattuglia vigilanza terrestre avanzata

    5ª Compagnia Sahariana, with:

        17ª squadra di pilotaggio zone desertiche reparto celere

    6ª Compagnia Sahariana, with:

        pattuglia vigilanza terrestre avanzata (from 2ª Compagnia Sahariana)

    Batteria di Formazione Sahariana (training battery)

    839ª Batteria da 77/28

    844ª Batteria da 77/28

Note:
– The *7ª Compagnia Sahariana is reported as being formed from July 1942, but afterwards it disappears from the orders of battle*

in the area between Fort Lamy and Khartoum. He also changed his defensive tactics so that the *Compagnie Sahariane* continuously patrolled the vast areas separating Italian garrisons. Permission to create desert-raiding parties was granted on 10 July and, after facing many difficulties in finding suitable vehicles, Piatti Dal Pozzo finally managed to form the first Pattuglia Vigilanza Terrestre Avanzata (advanced land surveillance patrol) on 30 September 1942, attached to the 5ª Compagnia Sahariana; followed by patrol number 2 on 8 October (with 3ª Compagnia Sahariana) and finally by patrols number 3 and 4 on 15 October (both with 2ª Compagnia Sahariana). Two Squadre di Pilotaggio Zone Desertiche (desert navigation schools) were set up in June and on 4 November a nucleus of 21 Arditi from the 103ª Compagnia Arditi Camionettisti (the Italian equivalent of the Commandos) arrived at Hon to start their training, scheduled to be over by mid-December 1942. Four days later the first eight of the new AS42 Sahariana finally arrived and were used to equip patrol No. 3 at Zella, which was promptly renamed Reparto Celere 3 (fast-moving unit) and merged with the Arditi. Reparto Celere 3 was used for patrolling and had its first clashes with an LRDG patrol on 17 November, when it lost one Sahariana, and on 25 November, when it succeeded in destroying four out of the eight enemy vehicles it encountered.

However, the tide of the desert war had turned against the Italians and in December General Alberto Mannerini, (who on 24 October had taken over the Comando del Sahara Libico from Piatti Dal Pozzo) started the Italian retreat from the Fezzan. Pressed by the Free French, Mannerini also faced the gradual disruption of the Libyan troops. The *Compagnie Sahariane* were brought up to strength using all the Italian soldiers evacuated from the Sahara, and survived and formed the core of the Raggruppamento Mannerini (also known as Raggruppamento Sahariano) along with the 15ª R.E.Co. Cavalleggeri di Lodi (Armoured Recce Group) and the 3ª Compagnia PAI. In February the Raggruppamento Sahariano was further increased to a total of six battalions, about 5,000 men. This unit fought hard in Tunisia, till the final surrender in May 1943.

A patrol of Sahariana moving in the desert. Their long range, four-wheel drive and heavy firepower made these vehicles perfectly suited to this difficult environment. (Filippo Cappellano – AUSSME)

A Fiat 500 Coloniale and an AS37 truck. These two vehicles were among the most effective Italian vehicles used in desert operations, although the Fiat 500 Coloniale lacked traction and horsepower and was clearly inferior to the American Willys jeep and the German Kübelwagen. (Filippo Cappellano – AUSSME)

Free French forces

The Forces Françaises Libres (FFL) were instigated in Britain in late June 1940, their cadre provided by some 1,300 men of the Corps expéditionnaire français en Scandinavie (French Expeditionary Corps in Scandinavia). Raising this force from scratch proved to be a difficult task for General Charles de Gaulle, who had to rely a wide extent on the Légion étrangère – the renowned French Foreign Legion – to expand the forces at his disposal. On 2 July 1940, the 1ère brigade de légion française (BLE) was raised in Britain, though its strength remained depressingly low: by mid-August it had only 2,721 all ranks, of which 103 were officers. It is therefore unsurprising that the bulk of the Free French forces came from France's colonial armies. This is what happened in Chad, which was the first major French colony to join de Gaulle's Free France on 26 August 1940, where Lieutenant-Colonel D'Ornano quickly turned the local Régiment de tirailleurs sénégalais du Tchad (RTST) into the main Free French combat force in Equatorial Africa. The only help de Gaulle could send was his delegate to the French Equatorial Africa colonies, Captain Viscount Philippe de Hauteclocque, who changed his name to Philippe Leclerc after he had joined de Gaulle. Promoted to the rank of major, he successfully organized bloodless coups in the French colonies of Cameroon (27 August) and Congo (28 August). Leclerc also successfully led the Free French Forces in their campaign against the Vichy French forces in Gabon in October–November 1940. All that was achieved mainly thanks to the availability of the colonial Régiment de tirailleurs sénégalais du Tchad, which was to supply the cadre of the only Free French units that were to fight independently during World War II in a theatre of war: the Saharan region of the Fezzan.

The RTST was more like a police force than an infantry regiment, as its main purpose was internal security. It had its HQ, services, depot and three infantry companies at Fort Lamy (today N'Djamena), where Leclerc established his own HQ on 2 December 1940, when he took over local command from D'Ornano. The total strength of the regiment was 6,133 all ranks, of which only 469 were Europeans. The regiment was organized in a standard colonial fashion; apart from its HQ battalion, it consisted of four different *groupes* (groups – roughly equivalent to a battalion) deployed in four different regions: Groupe I at Fort Archambault (three infantry coys plus one depot), Groupe II at Abéché (three infantry and one mounted coys, plus one depot), Groupe III at Largeau (four infantry coys, one motorized company and four mounted groups) and Groupe IV at Mao (four infantry and two mounted coys, one depot plus one group and two mounted sections). Groupe III was the most mobile and best equipped and it included the only motorized unit available – the compagnie portée – and four camel-mounted groups. Three of these groups were suitable for operations outside their assigned area or in the Fezzan: the Groupe nomade de l'Ennedi (GNE), the Groupe nomade du Borkou (GNB) and the Groupe nomade du Tibesti (GNT). Leclerc understood at once how important motorized units were if he wanted to wage war against the Italians in the desert and, soon after his

A French motorized column travelling in the Fezzan at the end of 1942. With the Axis forces retreating after the battle of El Alamein, the Free French occupied southern Libya. (Memorial Leclerc)

arrival in Chad on 2 December 1940, he selected the best units available to form a mobile force. By the end of the month the Colonne Leclerc began to take shape, though initially as a sub-unit of the RTST. The column was formed around the compagnie portée and the 7e compagnie du RTST, both later transformed into *compagnies de découverte et de combat* (DC, reconnaissance and combat companies), plus the GNE and other support units, including an artillery section of the RTST armed with two 75mm mountain guns (**Fig. 21**).

Between January and February 1941 only about 460 men were engaged in the Free French's first actions: ten (including five Europeans) joined the LRDG on its raid on Murzuk, 48 (only three Europeans) took part in the raid against

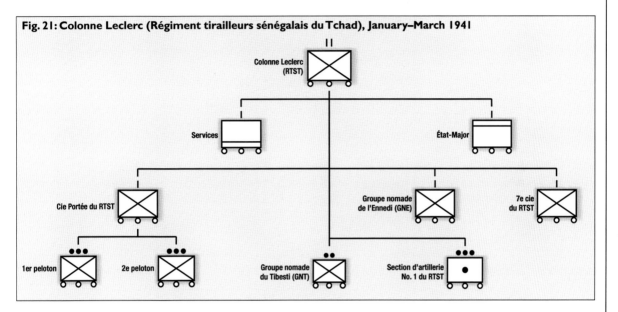

Fig. 21: Colonne Leclerc (Régiment tirailleurs sénégalais du Tchad), January–March 1941

Table 13: Colonne Leclerc (Régiment de tirailleurs sénégalais du Tchad), January – March 1941

	Strength (French/Native)	Vehicles	Heavy weapons
État-Major	11/7	1 x Brak Matford; 2 x Chevrolet pick up; 1 x Austin; 2 x Bedford*	
Compagnie portée du RTST **			
1er peloton de Combat	20	6 x Bedford	2 x 37mm guns
2e peloton de Combat	20	6 x Bedford	2 x 8mm HMGs
Groupe nomade de l'Ennedi	14/96	1 x Dodge pick up; 16 x Matford l'Ennedi (GNE)	
7e compagnie du RTST	9/69	1 x Dodge pick up; 8 x Matford	
Groupe nomade du Tibesti (GNT) – detachment	3	1 x Dodge pick up; 1 x Bedford	
Section d'artillerie No. 1 du RTST	5/16	4 Laffly; 1 x Dodge pick up; 2 x Matford; 1 x Bedford	2 Mod. 28 75mm mountain artillery pieces
Services	22/67	102 light and heavy lorries	
Total	104/255		

* one of which was equipped with a radio
** reduced strength; originally each Peloton had 43/45 and 23 Bedford lorries

A Bedford truck in service with French forces heavily laden with supplies. The vehicle is armed with a Hotchkiss machine gun and a 7.5mm light machine gun. (Memorial Leclerc)

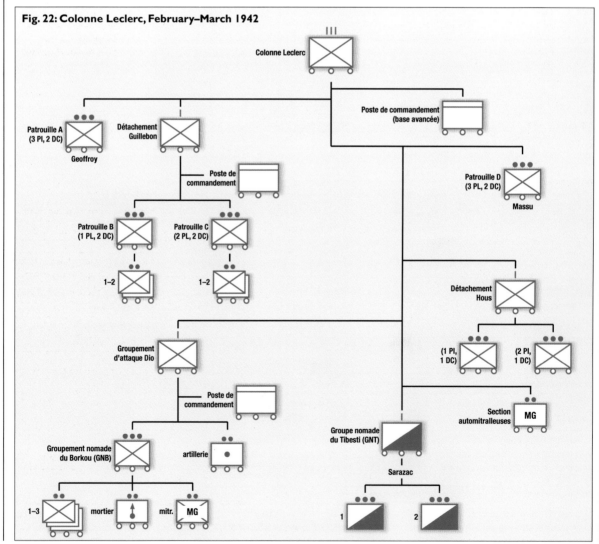

Fig. 22: Colonne Leclerc, February–March 1942

Colonne Leclerc

Poste de commandement (base avancée)

Patrouille A (3 Pl, 2 DC) — Geoffroy

Détachement Guillebon

Poste de commandement

Patrouille D (3 PL, 2 DC) — Massu

Patrouille B (1 PL, 2 DC)

Patrouille C (2 PL, 2 DC)

1–2

1–2

Détachement Hous

(1 PI, 1 DC)

(2 PI, 1 DC)

Groupement d'attaque Dio

Poste de commandement

Section automitralleuses — MG

Groupement nomade du Borkou (GNB)

artillerie

Groupe nomade du Tibesti (GNT) — Sarazac

1–3

mortier

mitr. MG

1

2

Tejerri and 402 (101 Europeans, 295 native and six native scouts) were in the column that attacked Kufra. These low numbers were partly due to the use of a large number of men to move supplies supplies from the bases in Chad up to the Tibesti, the mountain region that borders the Fezzan. The transport columns succeeded in moving all the supplies needed from Douala (a port in French Cameroon) to Fort Archambauld and Fort Lamy, and from there up to Uigh el Kebir – a journey of around 4,000km across harsh terrain.

Soon after the seizure of Kufra, the Colonne Leclerc was reorganized and expanded, though its combat strength remained steady at around 500, plus some other 400 extra in the rear area. The two *compagnies* DC were broken down into single *pelotons* (platoons), which – following the example of the Long Range Desert Group – formed desert *patrouilles*; each patrol included two sections equipped with about twelve lorries. The former compagnie portée, renamed 2e compagnie DC, provided the cadres for Patrouilles A, B and C, the latter two grouped together to form the Détachement Guillebon – roughly the equivalent of an LRDG squadron. The third platoon of the 7e compagnie du RTST formed Patrouille D, while the two other platoons formed the Détachement Hous, named after its commander. Support was provided by the Groupement d'attaque Dio, formed around the Groupe nomade du Borkou, which had exchanged its camels for motor vehicles, and by Capitaine Sarazac's Groupe nomade du Tibesti (**Fig. 22**). British supplies and Italian captured equipment had also greatly improved the weapons allocation. However, the first raid in the Fezzan ended with failure for the Colonne Leclerc, due to the reinforcement of the Italian forces in the area and it was clear that the Colonne needed further strengthening if it was to make any impact.

Between March and November 1942, Leclerc busied himself with the task of improving the strength and fighting power of his forces. A higher degree of motorization was made possible thanks to the acquisition of British and American vehicles and by December 1942 the Colonne possessed 787 motor vehicles. In summer 1942 reinforcements also arrived in the form of the bataillon de marche No. 3 (march battalion), formerly part of the 1ère division d'infanterie that had fought in Syria, which was disbanded to supply cadres for the RTST. By December 1942 the Colonne Leclerc had reached regimental size,

Leclerc, the head of the Free French forces in Chad, addressing his troops. His real name was Philippe de Hauteclocque. A charismatic and inspiring leader, he was eager to fight a genuinely 'French' war, with Free French forces playing the prominent role. (Memorial Leclerc)

Table 14: Colonne Leclerc, February–March 1942			
	Strength	Vehicles	Heavy weapons
Patrouille A (Cne. André Geoffroy)	40	12 x Chevrolet	1 x 20mm Oerlikon; 1 x 60mm Brandt mortar; 1 x 12.7mm Breda HMG; 1 x MAC MG; 7 x 8mm Hotchkiss MG; 1 x 13.2mm Hotchkiss HMG; 2 x AT rifles
Détachement Guillebon (Cne. Jacques de Guillebon)	66	24 x Chevrolet; 12 x Ford	3 x 20mm Oerlikon; 9 x 8mm Hotchkiss MG; 2 x 81mm mortar; 1 AT rifle
Patrouille D (Cne. Massu)	40	15 x Bedford	
Groupement Dio (Cdt. Louis Dio)	70	1 x Ford pick up; 20 x Chevrolet; 2 x Bedford pick up; 5 x Matford	1 45-pdr howitzer
Détachement Hous (Cdt. Hous)	60	24 x Bedford; 3 x SPA	2 x 20mm guns; 2 x 81mm mortars; 1 x 37mm gun; 2 x 13.2mm Hotchkiss HMG
Groupe nomade du Tibesti (Cne. Maurice Sarrazac)	120		2 x 13.2mm Hotchkiss HMG
Section automitralleuses	?	3 x Marmon-Herrington, each with 1 x Boys AT rifle	

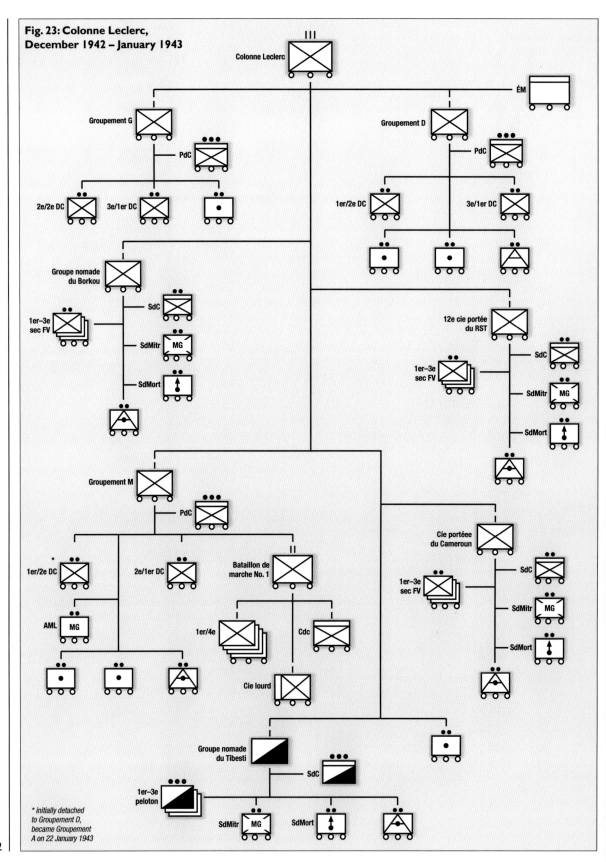

Fig. 23: Colonne Leclerc,
December 1942 – January 1943

Colonne Leclerc

ÉM

Groupement G

PdC

2e/2e DC   3e/1er DC

Groupement D

PdC

1er/2e DC   3e/1er DC

Groupe nomade
du Borkou

SdC

1er–3e
sec FV

SdMitr   MG

SdMort

12e cie portée
du RST

SdC

1er–3e
sec FV

SdMitr   MG

SdMort

Groupement M

PdC

1er/2e DC *   2e/1er DC   Bataillon de
marche No. 1

AML   MG

1er/4e   Cdc

Cie lourd

Cie portée
du Cameroun

SdC

1er–3e
sec FV

SdMitr   MG

SdMort

Groupe nomade
du Tibesti

SdC

1er–3e
peloton

SdMitr   MG   SdMort

* initially detached
to Groupement D,
became Groupement
A on 22 January 1943

42

Table 15: Colonne Leclerc December 1942–January 1943

État-Major – Général Philippe Leclerc

    Cellule radio Leclerc

    Cellule radio Ingold

    LRDG S2 Patrol (attached)

    Section d'artillerie (SA 12)

Groupement G – Capitaine André Geoffroy

    Poste de Commandement

    2e peloton de 2e DC

    3e peloton de 1er DC

    Section d'artillerie (SA 11)

Groupement D – Lieutenant-Colonel Louis Dio

    Poste de commandement

    1er peloton de 2e DC

    3e peloton de 1er DC

    Section d'artillerie (SA 11, SA 15 bis)

    1er–2e demi-section d'artillerie antiaérienne

Groupe nomade du Borkou (GNB)

    Section de commandement

    1er section de fusiliers voltigeurs

    2e section de fusiliers voltigeurs

    3e section de fusiliers voltigeurs

    Groupe d'accompagnement

        Section de mitralleuses

        Section de mortiers

        Section AA et AC (Artillerie Antiaérienne et Anti Chars)

12e compagnie portée du RTST

    Section de commandement

    1er section de fusiliers voltigeurs

    2e section de fusiliers voltigeurs

    3e section de fusiliers voltigeurs

    Groupe d'accompagnement

        Section de mitralleuses

        Section de mortiers

        Section AA et AC

Groupement M – Lieutenant-Colonel Delange

    Poste de commandement

    1er peloton de 2e DC

    2e peloton de 1er DC

    Bataillon de marche No. 1

        Compagnie de commandement

        1er compagnie

        2e compagnie

(continues on page 44)

3e compagnie

4e compagnie

Compagnie lourde

Section d'automitralleuses

Section d'artillerie (SA 16 bis, SA 11)

Section AA et AC (SA 29)

Compagnie portée du Cameroun

Section de commandement

1er section de fusiliers voltigeurs

2e section de fusiliers voltigeurs

3e section de fusiliers voltigeurs

Groupe d'accompagnement

Section de mitralleuses

Section de mortiers

Section AA et AC

Groupe nomade du Tibesti (GNT)

Section de commandement

1er section de fusiliers voltigeurs

2e section de fusiliers voltigeurs

3e section de fusiliers voltigeurs

Groupe d'accompagnement

Section de mitralleuses

Section de mortiers

Section AA et AC

with a combat strength of 2,758 (510 Europeans) divided into three *groupements* and a support *groupe* (groups), two *compagnies portées* and the Groupe nomade du Tibesti (total strength was of 4,735, with some 2,000 in the rear area). Leclerc had also reorganized his units internally, turning them into effective combat groups that included *sections d'artillerie* (artillery sections), *sections de mitralleuses* or *automitralleuses* (machine-gun or armoured cars sections), *sections de mortiers* (mortar sections) and *sections artillerie antiaérienne et anti chars* (anti-aircraft and anti-tank sections). Groupements G (Capitaine Geoffroy), D (Lieutenant-Colonel Dio) and M (Lieutenant-Colonel Delange) were an improvement over the former *patrouilles*, while the 12e compagnie portée du RTST and the Compagnie portée du Cameroun were, like the Groupe nomade du Borkou, motorized colonial units. The camel-mounted Groupe nomade du Tibesti, the large supply services and air support were also included to provide support to the leading troops. On 23 December 1942, while the Axis forces were retreating from El Alamein, the three *groupements* of the Colonne Leclerc began the second French campaign in the Fezzan. Their first target was the capture of Um el Araneb (26 December–4 January 1943) followed by Gatrun (1–6 January 1943), both of which were tenaciously defended by Italian troops. On 9 January 1943 the Italians began to withdraw from the Fezzan (as part of the general retreat from Libya), and the Free French forces started their pursuit. Hon was seized on 13 January, and finally Tripoli was reached on the 26th where contact was established with Eighth Army and the Free French unit advancing from the east, the *colonne volante* (flying column) of Commandant Rémy, which was absorbed by Leclerc's forces. Soon after, the Colonne Leclerc was renamed Force L and, at the conclusion of the Tunisian campaign, it provided the cadres of the 2e division blindée (2nd Armoured Division).

German forces

German forces in North Africa were continuously plagued by supply and manpower issues, which affected their first attempt to set up a desert-raiding force. As early as March 1941, the German Army High Command (OKH) passed on to Rommel a proposal made by Hauptmann von Homeyer, an officer with desert-travelling experience, concerning the creation of a small desert-raiding patrol. With this patrol based around six Kübelwagen and a total crew of 12, von Homeyer intended to travel deep into the desert going via Kufra and Auwenat before reaching the Nile Valley at Derut. Authorization to form the Verband Homeyer was granted in late March but, due to transportation difficulties across the Mediterranean, it does not appear to have reached Libya until early 1942. Following this date its whereabouts are unknown and it can only be assumed that it was attached to the Brandenburgers or Sonderkommando Dora.

Other German special forces faced similar problems and, more than often, these units ended up fighting at the front. This is certainly the case with the Sonderverband (Special Formation) 288, which was formed on 24 July 1941 in the wake of the experiences of Sonderstab Felmy (Special Staff Felmy) in Iraq during the doomed uprising of May 1941. Sonderverband 288 was a strong unit (**Fig. 24**) and included a company of Brandenburgers, three different infantry companies, an anti-tank company (with a Sturmgeschütz platoon), an anti-aircraft company and an assault engineer company. It also had many 'specialists' including a group of officers who spoke Arabic. The unit was sent to Greece in autumn 1941 to complete its training and in January 1942 it began to be transferred to North Africa. A nucleus of about 400 men, known as Kampfgruppe Menton after its commander Oberst Otto Menton, was attached to 90.leichte Afrika Division

Two members of the Sonderkommando Dora and their Kübelwagen. The unit insignia (a red scorpion on a white shield) is painted on the right mudguard. The Kübelwagen was the only German vehicle that proved suited to desert operations. This lack of suitable vehicles hampered the development of German unconventional operations in North Africa. (Memorial Leclerc)

Table 16: Sonderverband 288, May 1942
Stabskompanie – Aufklärungszug (mounted on Kübelwagen. 7 LMGs); Panzerspähwagen Zug (3 armoured cars SdKfz 222)
Sturmgeschütz Zug (attached from 5. Kompanie, 3 Sturmgeschütz)
Nachrichtenkompanie – 4 LMGs, 2 HMGs
2. Gebirgsjäger Kompanie – HQ, anti-tank and mortar sections, 3 infantry platoons (each with HQ, 4 infantry squads and a mortar section), maintenance section and trains (13 LMGs, 2 AT rifles, 3 AT guns 50mm, 3 light mortars, 2 heavy mortars)
3. Schützen Kompanie – same as 2. Kompanie (13 LMGs, 2 AT rifles, 3 AT guns 50mm, 3 light mortars, 2 heavy mortars)
4. Maschinengewehr Kompanie – HQ, 2 MG platoons (each with HQ and 3 MG sections), 1 mortar platoon on 3 sections, maintenance section and trains (1 LMG, 12 HMGs, 3 AT guns 37mm, 6 heavy mortars)
5. Panzerjäger Kompanie – HQ, 2 AT platoons 37mm, 1 AT platoon 50mm, maintenance section and trains (4 LMGs, 6 AT guns 37mm, 3 AT guns 50mm; later 9 captured AT guns 42mm)
6. Fla Kompanie – HQ, signals detachment, 3 AA platoons, maintenance section and trains (4 LMGs, 2 AT rifles, 12 selfpropelled AA guns 20mm)
7. Pionier Kompanie – HQ, signals section, 3 engineers platoons, maintenance section and trains (11 LMGs, 2 AT rifles, 3 AT guns 37mm, 3 light mortars)
Leichte Kolonne – (2 LMGs)
Sanitäts Staffel – (2 LMGs)
Werkstatt Zug – (1 LMG)

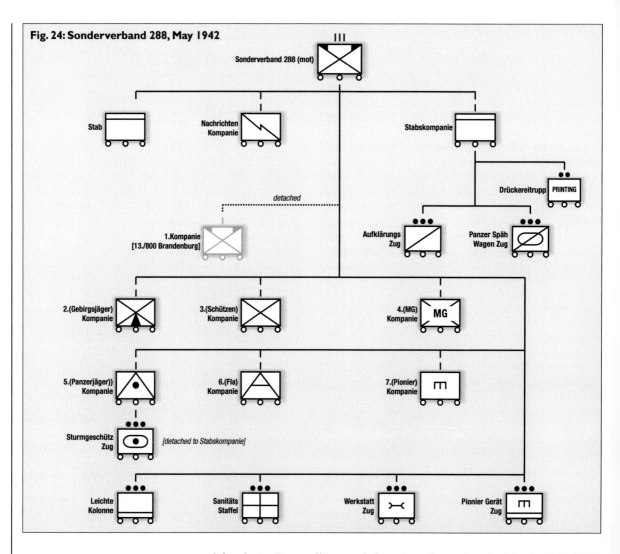

Fig. 24: Sonderverband 288, May 1942

Sonderverband 288 (mot)

Stab

Nachrichten Kompanie

Stabskompanie

Drückereitrupp PRINTING

detached

1.Kompanie [13./800 Brandenburg]

Aufklärungs Zug

Panzer Späh Wagen Zug

2.(Gebirgsjäger) Kompanie

3.(Schützen) Kompanie

4.(MG) Kompanie MG

5.(Panzerjäger)) Kompanie

6.(Fla) Kompanie

7.(Pionier) Kompanie

Sturmgeschütz Zug

[detached to Stabskompanie]

Leichte Kolonne

Sanitäts Staffel

Werkstatt Zug

Pionier Gerät Zug

and fought in Rommel's second drive into Cyrenaica. By March 1942 1,400 personnel were still outstanding (Sonderverband 288 was 1,800 strong), along with most of the 610 vehicles and heavy weapons. The transportation of the unit was finally completed by May, though by then it had lost much of its special forces status. The specialists had been left in Greece with Sonderstab Felmy while 1.Kompanie, 13./Lehr Regiment Brandenburg, was detached for special duties. Sonderverband 288 fought as a regular infantry unit (in May–June 1942 it became part of Kampfgruppe Hecker and fought at Bir Hacheim, then at Mersa Matruh and El Alamein), first attached to 90.leichte Afrika Division and then, from February 1943, to 164.leichte Afrika Division. In July 1942 its organization changed to that of a two-battalion regiment and in August Panzerarmee Afrika ordered that it was to change its designation into that of Panzer Grenadier Regiment Afrika, an order that was eventually carried out on 31 October.

A similar fate also befell 13./Lehr Regiment Brandenburg, also known as the Tropen Kompanie (Tropical Company). This unit was formed in May 1942 under the command of the Oberleutnant Friedrich von Koenen and had a structure similar to that of the other Brandenburger companies (**Fig. 25**, total strength was about 300). From late October it had a *Halb-Kompanie* (half company) in Greece with Sonderverband 288 and a second one stationed in Italy, at Naples. The former, probably with the schwere Zug, was sent to North

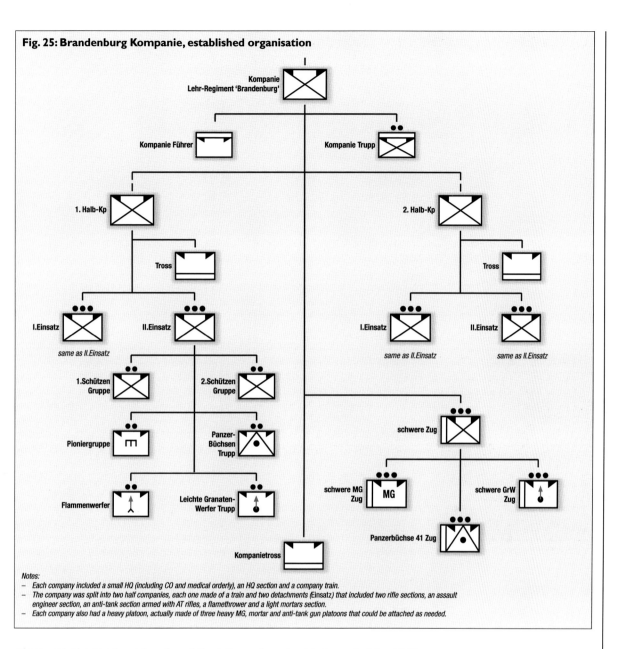

Fig. 25: Brandenburg Kompanie, established organisation

Kompanie
Lehr-Regiment 'Brandenburg'

Kompanie Führer

Kompanie Trupp

1. Halb-Kp

2. Halb-Kp

Tross

Tross

I.Einsatz

II.Einsatz

I.Einsatz

II.Einsatz

same as II.Einsatz

same as II.Einsatz

same as II.Einsatz

1.Schützen Gruppe

2.Schützen Gruppe

Pioniergruppe

Panzer-Büchsen Trupp

schwere Zug

Flammenwerfer

Leichte Granaten-Werfer Trupp

schwere MG Zug

MG

schwere GrW Zug

Panzerbüchse 41 Zug

Kompanietross

Notes:
- Each company included a small HQ (including CO and medical orderly), an HQ section and a company train.
- The company was split into two half companies, each one made of a train and two detachments (Einsatz) that included two rifle sections, an assault engineer section, an anti-tank section armed with AT rifles, a flamethrower and a light mortars section.
- Each company also had a heavy platoon, actually made of three heavy MG, mortar and anti-tank gun platoons that could be attached as needed.

Africa with the Sonderverband, and the latter only arrived in June. In May 1942 the Kompanie von Koenen (as the half company was then known) was attached to Kampfgruppe Hecker, which also included the third battalion of the Italian 'San Marco' marine regiment and the Pionier Landungs Kompanie 778. The latter, equipped with landing barges, was intended to land the Brandenburgers and the Italian marines behind the British defence line at Gazala to assault the Via Balbia while Rommel launched his attack south of Bir Hacheim. The seaborne operation was not carried out. Instead on 29 May Kampfgruppe Hecker was moved to Bir Hacheim and, reinforced with Rommel's Kampfstaffel (combat detachment), attacked the French-held fortress. The company fought as a special reconnaissance force with the Afrika Korps until El Alamein, after which it withdrew to Tunisia to became part of von Koenen's battalion.

The Abwehr (German intelligence service) was the only German service that successfully created a desert-raiding force, and this owed much to a fortuitous

Sonderkommando von Almaszy travelling in the desert. Operation *Salaam* was the only operation of this kind performed by German forces and provides an indication of what could have been achieved if the Germans had been more far-sighted with their desert operations. (Carlo Pecchi)

meeting in Budapest between an Abwehr officer and Count Ladislas (Laszlo) von Almaszy, a former major in the Austrian Army whose desert-going experience matched that of Bagnold.

Following the German intervention in North Africa, the chief of the Abwehr, Admiral Canaris, ordered the Luftwaffe's Major Nikolaus Ritter (chief of the Luftwaffe's section of the Abwehr I department, espionage) to form a Sonderkommando (special unit) for special operations in North Africa. The main task of this unit was to infiltrate German spies into Egypt and to establish contact with the chief-of-staff of the Egyptian Army, el Masri Pasha. Despite von Almaszy's advice, Ritter decided to use aircraft to infiltrate these agents and the attempts ended in repeated failure until 16 July 1941, when Ritter was wounded after one of the aircraft crash-landed. Six months later, on 26 January 1942, the German General Staff (OKW) authorized the creation of a special unit, named Sonderkommando Dora. Put under the command of Panzerarmee Afrika's Abwehr officer, Oberstleutnant Walter Eichler, the Sonderkommando Dora included a number of specialists such as geologists, cartographers and mineralogists, who were intended to provide support for the unit's special mission, which consisted of deep raiding and infiltration in the desert.

Even before Sonderkommando Dora had established itself in the desert, von Almaszy carried out his own mission. On 11 May 1942 his own Sonderverband carried out Operation *Condor*, which infiltrated two German spies into Egypt. Although quite strong and well equipped, Sonderkommando Dora (with 19 officers, 18 NCOs and 56 enlisted men) was poorly suited for operations in the deep desert (**Fig. 26**). With the exception of the Kübelwagen, its vehicles were not suited to the conditions in the Sahara and they lacked adequate range and speed. Their aircraft were also of little use apart from the delivery of supplies. It is probably for this reason that they focused their attention towards the weaker Free French forces in Chad, although the orders from Berlin clearly stated that Egypt was to be their main theatre of operations. Nevertheless, in early July two patrols were organized, the first with one heavy Horch staff car, three Kübelwagen and two Opel trucks (a strength of eight officers, three NCOs and 14 enlisted men), the second with four Kübelwagen and a single Opel truck (a strength of six officers, six NCOs and six enlisted men). For three weeks they carried out a long-range patrol in the Fezzan, mostly to acquire experience that was later used by the second half company of Brandenburgers. This unit was mustered in Tripoli in mid-June and, after the capture of Tobruk (and of large quantities of booty), had been equipped with suitable British-made vehicles. Under the command of Oberleutnant Conrad von Leipzig, the unit was about 100 strong and was equipped with 24 British vehicles (half of which were armed with 40mm guns), four jeeps, a command and a radio truck plus many other trucks for supplies; they even had a Spitfire fighter to provide air protection. In early July, after a two-week period of preparation, the unit began its march toward Murzuk, where it arrived by mid-July. There it split

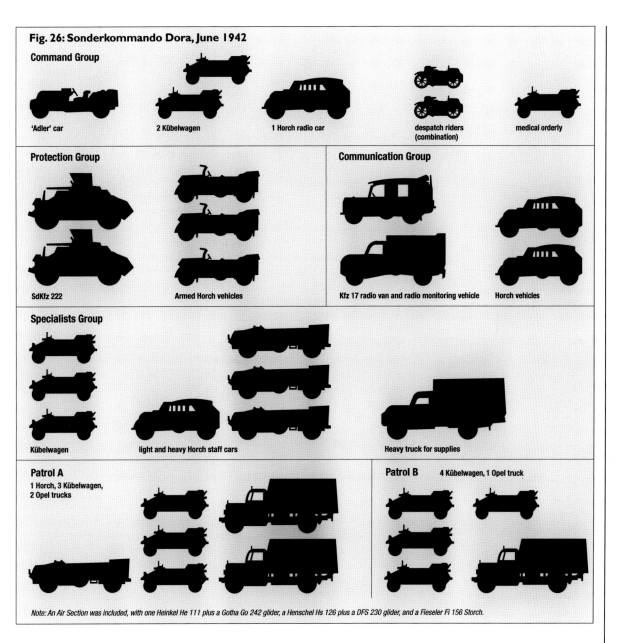

Fig. 26: Sonderkommando Dora, June 1942

Command Group

'Adler' car　　2 Kübelwagen　　1 Horch radio car　　despatch riders (combination)　　medical orderly

Protection Group

SdKfz 222　　Armed Horch vehicles

Communication Group

Kfz 17 radio van and radio monitoring vehicle　　Horch vehicles

Specialists Group

Kübelwagen　　light and heavy Horch staff cars　　Heavy truck for supplies

Patrol A
1 Horch, 3 Kübelwagen,
2 Opel trucks

Patrol B　　4 Kübelwagen, 1 Opel truck

Note: An Air Section was included, with one Heinkel He 111 plus a Gotha Go 242 glider, a Henschel Hs 126 plus a DFS 230 glider, and a Fieseler Fi 156 Storch.

into three with two patrols heading for Chad and a third patrol heading west to Algeria. While training, Sonderkommando Dora also supported the Italian defence of the Sahara, setting up two reconnaissance patrols to work in the Hon area. In November 1942, following the Axis retreat from El Alamein, both Sonderkommando Dora and the Brandenburgers were withdrawn from the Sahara. The former was eventually disbanded on 21 January 1943, the latter joined the Abteilung von Koenen to fight in Tunisia.

Tactics

The desert fighting of 1940–43 was a new kind of warfare and required the development of new tactics. The first, basic mission of the Long Range Desert Patrol in September 1940 was to reconnoitre approach routes to enemy territory and to establish supply dumps along the main roads. Once inside hostile territory, the LRDP's tactics varied according to the mission. The primary mission of long-range penetration was reconnaissance. This covered both the terrain and the enemy's defensive lines. The LRDP missions were the only realistic way of obtaining information about the Italian defences in the Sahara, as air reconnaissance proved useless and there were no spies or informers in the area. These missions were to avoid any contact with enemy forces. A secondary LRDP role was to harass the enemy's lines of communication and destroy suitable targets like supply dumps. These missions relied on speed and surprise for their success, and the LRDP could not take an offensive role in the face of a determined defence.

In November 1940 a decision was taken for the LRDG, along with the Free French forces in Chad, to undertake a series of offensive operations against Italian posts in southern Libya. These early missions help to illustrate how the unit's tactics actually developed.

The LRDG in the Fezzan, 27 December 1940–9 February 1941

Designed to coincide with Lieutenant-General Richard O'Connor's offensive in the north (Operation *Compass*), the LRDG's second operation (the first operation, actually a LRDP mission, started on 5 September 1940 and ended at the end of the same month and was predominantly a reconnaissance mission) was intended to test its capabilities as a 'nuisance' force, as well as to develop close cooperation with the Free French forces in Chad. Its results revealed some of the strengths and weaknesses of the LRDG as a combat force. T and G Patrols left Cairo on 27 November 1940 and reached Point A (south-east of Wau el Kebir) on 4 January 1941 having experienced no contact with the enemy. At this point Captain Clayton, commander of G Patrol, headed south to join the Free French at Kayugi, while T Patrol carried out reconnaissance to the east to survey the routes to the Kufra Oasis. Joined by a Free French group consisting of Lieutenant-Colonel d'Ornano and nine other men, the two patrols moved again on 8 January heading to Murzuk, which they reached three days later. It is worth noting that by this point the two LRDG patrols had covered about 2,200km kilometres since they left Cairo, and the Italians were still completely unaware of their presence. It should be remembered that by then the Italian defence forces had been stripped of most of their motorized units. There was only a single *Compagnia Sahariana* at Kufra that, along with the two other *Compagnie Mitraglieri*, was unmotorized and could not pursue the LRDG across open desert but was restricted to defending its own positions.

It is therefore unsurprising that the Italians' first reaction when they saw the approaching vehicles was to greet them with the Fascist salute, though, once they understood their mistake, the men of the 57ª Compagnia Mitraglieri set up a strong defence from inside the fort at Murzuk. The fighting lasted for over two hours, during which G Patrol, along with half of T Patrol and the Free French, seized the local airstrip and damaged the fort using a single 37mm Bofors gun and two 2in. mortars. The Italians returned

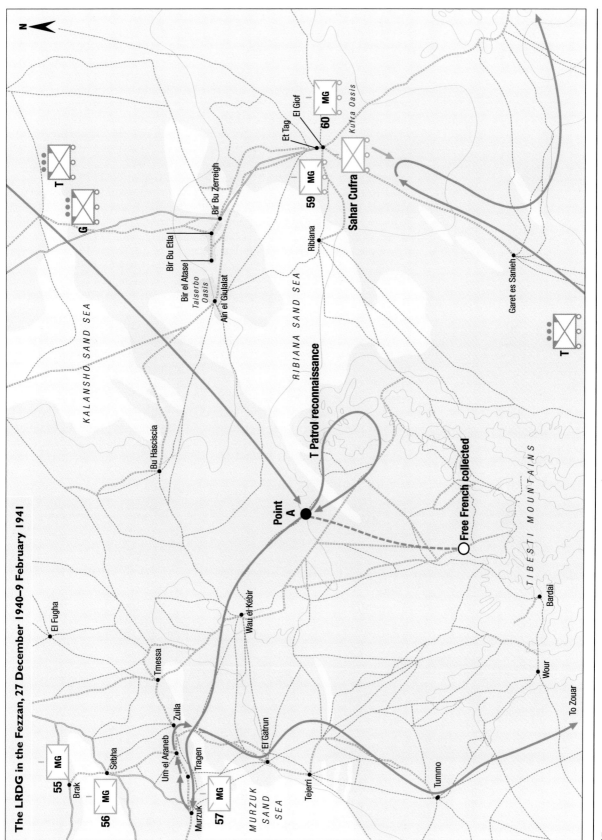

The LRDG in the Fezzan, 27 December 1940–9 February 1941

N

Kalansho Sand Sea

T

G

55 MG
56 MG

Brak

El Fugha

Sebha

Um el Araneb

57 MG

Murzuk

Murzuk Sand Sea

Tragen

Zuila

Tmessa

Wau el Kebir

El Gatrun

Tejerri

Tummo

To Zouar

Wour

Bardai

Tibesti Mountains

Free French collected

Point A

T Patrol reconnaissance

Ribiana Sand Sea

Bu Hasciscia

Ain el Giulalat

Taiserbo Oasis

Bir el Atase

Bir Bu Etla

Bir Bu Zerreigh

Ribiana

59 MG

Et Tag

El Giof

60 MG

Kufra Oasis

Sahar Cufra

T

Garet es Sanieh

fire, killing Lt. Col. d'Ornano and another man, and it became clear that the British and Free French forces were not strong enough to take the fort. In the afternoon the LRDG patrols moved away from Murzuk, heading first to Sebha and then westwards toward Tragen. The situation here was quite different as the village was only defended by two Italian *Carabinieri* (military police) who, taken completely by surprise, surrendered without attempting any kind of resistance. The villages of Um el Araneb and Gatrun were also garrisoned by a small force of *Carabinieri*, but they had been alerted to the presence of enemy forces and managed to defend their small strongpoints. The two patrols then headed south in the attempt to make contact with Captain Sarazac's Groupe nomade du Tibesti, although without success. The two groups eventually met further south, in the village of Zouar in Chad.

After a detour to the south, which included circling the Tibesti mountains, T and G Patrols split with the former heading north to reconnoitre the road to Kufra and the latter heading north-east toward the Libyan–Egyptian border at Uweinat. This time, however, the Italians were waiting for them. Having intercepted enemy radio signals from the south, on 28 January a patrol was formed from the Compagnia Sahariana at Kufra and sent to the south to check for any enemy. The column, some 40 strong and equipped with one AS 37 and four Fiat 634 lorries, zigzagged north of Bishara without encountering anything. Three days later T Patrol was sighted closing to Bishara by an Italian reconnaissance flight, which promptly alerted the *colonna mobile*, located just 65km from the Jebel Sherif where the LRDG patrol had stopped at 1130hrs. At 1400hrs the *colonna mobile* entered the Jebel Sherif to be greeted by heavy fire from T Patrol. The clash was brief but intense: three out of 11 LRDG vehicles were destroyed, one corporal was killed (along with two Italian prisoners taken at Murzuk) and four other soldiers missing (three of them eventually succeeded in making it back). The Italians lost one officer, Tenente Caputo, commander of the Compagnia Sahariana at Kufra, two Libyan soldiers and a single lorry. After a hurried retreat, the remnants of T Patrol – minus Captain Clayton and his crew of two, who were captured shortly later after their vehicle had been disabled by air attacks – escaped southwards to rejoin G Patrol for the long journey back to Egypt. The Italians proved unable to

A Caproni Ca309 Ghibli of the Aviazione Sahariana in flight. The tricolour painted on the rudder shows that this photo was taken before the outbreak of war. This light twin-engined aircraft could be used for liaison, observation or as a light bomber. Ghiblis were often the first to discover LRDG and Free French movements in the Sahara. (AUSSME)

pursue the LRDG because their vehicles were slower and the British force returned to Cairo on 9 February 1941 after a *c.*7,400km round trip.

Although not entirely successful, this first mission deep inside enemy territory provided useful experience. Bagnold's basic concepts proved sound, though tactics had to be refined. The first lesson learned was that LRDG patrols were too weak and poorly armed to successfully attack enemy garrisons, especially fortified positions. The second lesson was that, as soon as their presence was revealed, the LRDG patrols were too large and cumbersome to escape enemy reconnaissance, especially from the air. These drawbacks meant that the LRDG could not be a truly effective combat force; however, its successes in taking the enemy by surprise and its ability to move deeply behind the lines made it an effective raiding and reconnoitring force.

The Free French at Kufra, February 1941

The exploits of the LRDG did not completely rule out the old-fashioned form of desert warfare as the Free French action at Kufra reveals. After a temporary retreat following T Patrol's clash with the Italians, Colonel Leclerc, who had replaced d'Ornano, decided to attack the Italian garrison at Kufra on 5 February 1941. The forces at his disposal only consisted of the Compagnie portée of Captaine de Renneport (90 men and around 20 vehicles), who were later joined by the 120 men of the Compagnie nomade de l'Ennedi. Having approached

An LRDG portée. The truck is a Chevrolet 30-cwt and the gun is a 37mm Bofors. This vehicle took part in the attack on Murzuk on 11 January 1941. (Carlo Pecchi)

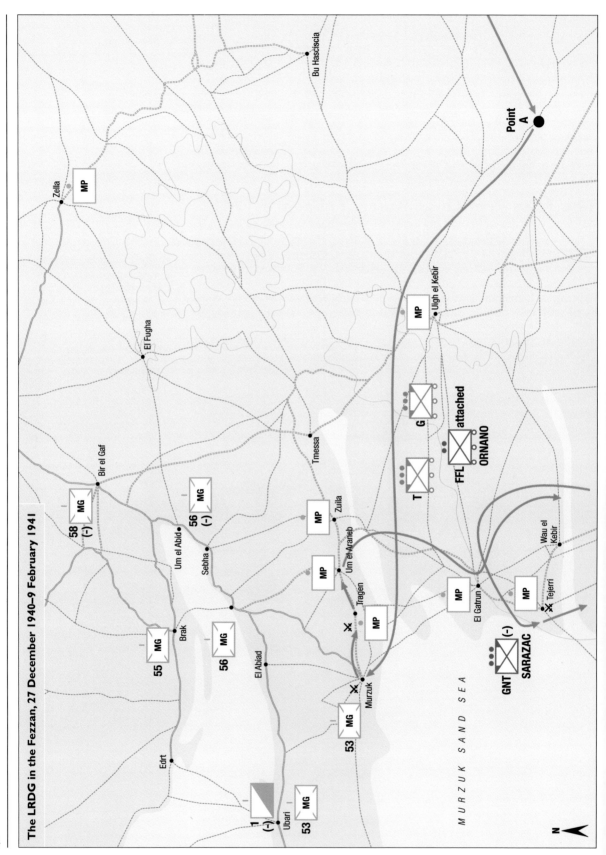

The LRDG in the Fezzan, 27 December 1940–9 February 1941

Point A

Bu Hasciscia

Zella MP

El Fugha

Ugh el Kebir MP

Bir el Gaf

Tmessa

G

58 (-) MG

56 (-) MG

T

FFL attached
ORNANO

Um el Abid

Sebha

55 MG

56 MG

Brak

El Abiad

Zuila MP

Um el Araneb MP

Tragen

MP

MP

Wau el Kebir

El Gatrun MP

MP Tejerri

GNT (-) SARAZAC

53 MG

Murzuk

53 MG

Edrt

Ubari

-1 (-)

MURZUK SAND SEA

N

54

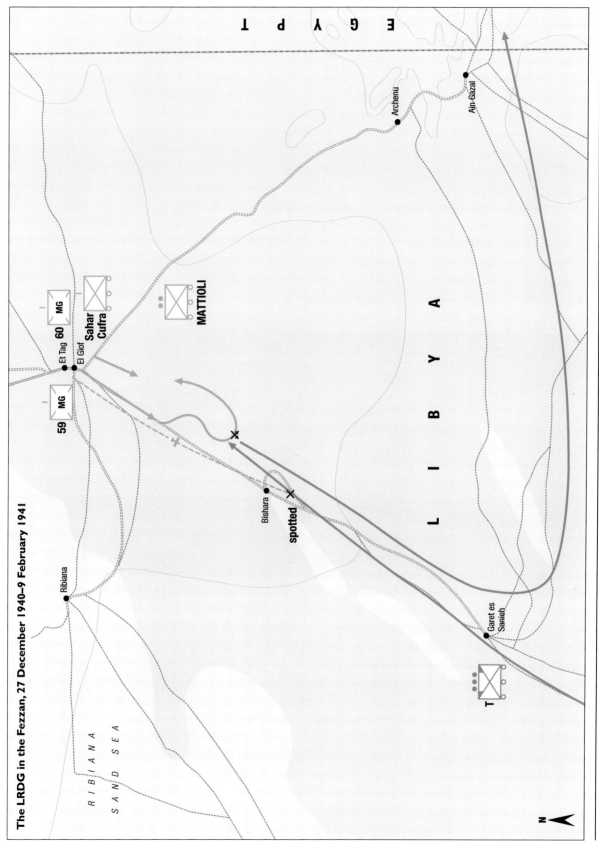

The LRDG in the Fezzan, 27 December 1940–9 February 1941

EGYPT

LIBYA

RIBIANA SAND SEA

Ribiana

Et Tag
El Giof
Sahar Cufra
60 MG
59 MG

MATTIOLI

Bishara
spotted

Archenu

Ain-Gazal

Garet es Sanieh

T

N

55

Eight TL37s were seized by the Colonne Leclerc after the surrender of the Italian garrison at Kufra. Once repaired, the TL37s were pressed into service with the French. (Memorial Leclerc)

French *carte postale* issued after the successful conquest of the Italian base of Kufra. The original caption reads: 'Enemy flag captured by the Régiment de tirailleurs sénégalais du Tchad at Kufra'. (Memorial Leclerc)

Kufra unseen, on the night of 7/8 February the two pelotons of the compagnie portée performed a successful raid against the Italian airstrip and withdrew without loss. The feeble reaction of the Italian garrison persuaded Leclerc to make an all-out attack in an attempt to seize the garrison and he assembled a force consisting of 100 French and 300 native soldiers, armed with four HMGs, two 37mm guns, four 81mm mortars and one 75mm gun. The French columns set out on 16 February and reached Kufra on the 18th. This time they were spotted by Italian aerial reconnaissance and the Italians organized another *colonna mobile* (70 strong, equipped with a captured Ford lorry, four Fiat 634 and ten AS37 lorries) which moved north of Kufra to meet the approaching Free French columns. The first clash between the Italians and the French was going the Italians' way, though the 1er peloton managed to outmanoeuvre the Italians on their left flank forcing them to withdraw north-north-west of the El Tag fort. The Italian garrison, composed of two Libyan *Compagnie Mitraglieri*, was surrounded and Leclerc blocked the roads to the north and south, while his guns begun to pound the Kufra fort.

On the 19th the *colonna mobile* returned to counterattack the French roadblock north-west of Kufra, while a bomber squadron attacked the Free French positions. The Italian attack was unsuccessful and, after two hours of fighting and in spite of negligible losses, the *colonna mobile* gave up and withdrew towards Taiserbo, unsuccessfully chased by the Free French. Meanwhile the Italian garrison at Kufra collapsed. They had lost their most experienced commander on 31 January, and his replacement had taken command of the *colonna mobile*. The garrison was now under the command of Capitano Colonna, a reserve officer who lacked both experience and nerve. After negotiations, the Italian garrison surrendered at midday on 1 March 1941. Eleven officers and 18 Italian other ranks were captured along with 273 Libyan soldiers; they had only lost three Libyan soldiers killed and four wounded. Kufra, the key to the Fezzan, had fallen into Free French hands and would have never be retaken by the Italians. Leclerc had won the last 'old-style' desert battle. The LRDG's raid into the Fezzan and the Free French seizure of Kufra were only first steps in the development of deep desert-raiding tactics. Leclerc's victory owed as much to good luck and Italian ineptitude as it did to the skill and bravery of his men. The coup succeeded thanks to the fact that Kufra was such an isolated position, and it is unsurprising that neither the Free French nor the LRDG ever achieved any similar success in the months to come.

Reconnaissance in Cyrenaica and Tripolitania

Between March and April 1941 the LRDG, minus A Squadron (G and Y Patrols), moved to Kufra, which Bagnold's men garrisoned together with Free French troops until July. This period saw the arrival of German troops in North Africa and Rommel's first drive into Cyrenaica and the LRDG saw little action, though A Squadron was active in reconnaissance. The use of LRDG patrols as reconnaissance units did have its limits. In April 1941, with Rommel's Afrikakorps leaping forward towards Tobruk, G Patrol had to abandon all its vehicles but one at Marada because of lack of fuel. Soon afterwards, A Squadron was forced to move eastwards from Jalo first to Jarabub and then to Siwa. The LRDG's area of operations area assigned on 30 March by Cyrenaica Command included an area stretching from Jarabub in the east to the oasis of Zella and Tagrifet in the west. However, the available patrols were mainly employed in other areas, sometimes with poor results. On 13/14 May 1941 what was left of G Patrol was sent to Sheferzen, some 8km north of Fort Maddalena, to perform an 'in-depth' reconnaissance along with the 11th Hussars; what they found there, however, was not the Hussars

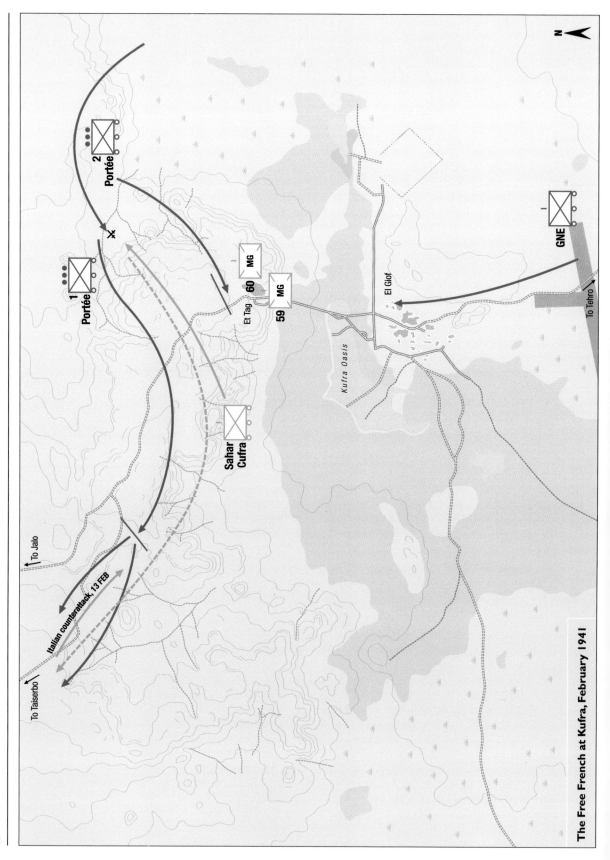

N

2 Portée

1 Portée

GNE

MG 60

MG 59

Et Tag

Sahar Cufra

El Giof

Kufra Oasis

To Jalo

To Taiserbo

Italian counterattack, 13 FEB

To Tehro

The Free French at Kufra, February 1941

Reconnaissance in Cyrenaica and Tripolitania

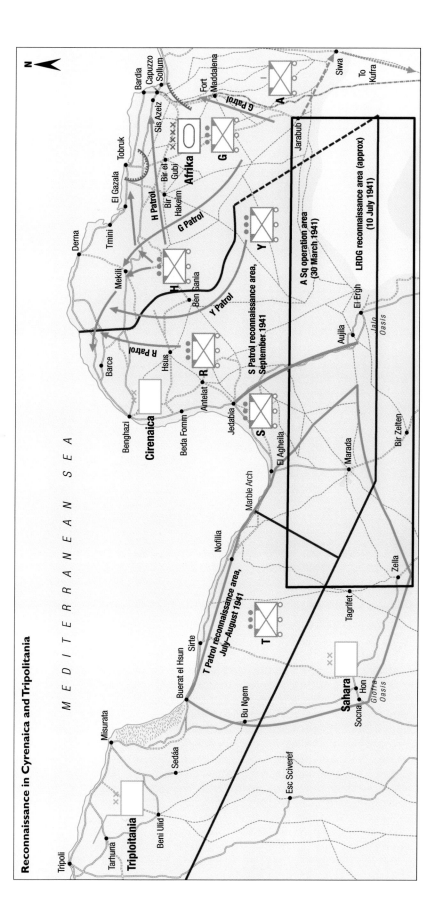

Men of the LRDG camouflage their vehicle to prevent detection from the air. Enemy aircraft were probably the most dangerous adversaries of the LRDG in the desert. (IWM, E 012403)

but rather German armoured troops who drove them off. This misuse of an LRDG patrol left G Patrol with only three trucks, and proved once more that the LRDG was not suitable for front-line action.

The stabilization of the front line, as well as the reorganization of A Squadron in June 1941, created once more the conditions that enabled the LRDG to be used at best, and the missions performed in June–July 1941 were deep desert raids, mainly connected with intelligence work. In June H Patrol's mission to Gambut (north-west of Bardia) succeeded in dropping two Arab agents behind enemy lines; later that month, another British intelligence officer and two Arabs were dropped east of Barce, while in early July two further Arab agents were dropped at Mersa Lukk, east of Tobruk. In mid-July, G Patrol returned to action and carried out reconnaissance in the Jebel Akhdar during which an enemy airstrip was raided. From late July Y Patrol also carried out reconnaissance in the Jebel Akhdar, though no raids. When compared to G Patrol's accident of mid-May, these missions were a total success: agents had been precisely dropped where asked, reconnaissance had been carried out well behind enemy lines, and the first attempts at raiding had been carried out successfully. The LRDG was on the right track and it was ready to widen its area of operations. T Patrol's 'in-depth' reconnaissance, carried out between the last

week of July and the first week of August, firmly established the basis of what would become the LRDG's standard method of practice.

The T Patrol reconnaissance area was not only wide, stretching along the El Agheila–Marada–Zella–Hon–Buerat el Hsun line and up north along the Via Balbia, but it was also deep inside Libya and well beyond the front line. Since reconnaissance was the main objective of the patrol, instructions stressed the importance of concealing movement from the enemy. This emphasis on concealment was a new departure for the LRDG, and from this point onwards contact with the enemy was only sought when conditions were completely in its favour. T Patrol's mission was a complete success. Although the patrol brought back no vital intelligence, it had travelled unseen deep into enemy territory thus confirming the soundness of the new tactics. S Patrol's reconnaissance of the Jalo–Jedabia road in early September, as well as R Patrol's mission in the Jebel Akhdar in August 1941 confirmed this was the way LRDG patrols needed to be employed. From October, these tactics proved particularly effective when the LRDG switched to another kind of activity, 'road watching'. This was intended to provide further intelligence on the movement of enemy troops close to its main supply harbour, Tripoli, and could only be carried out through strict concealment and avoidance of any contact with the enemy.

Vehicles of G Patrol prepare to leave Siwa. G Patrol was formed in 1940 from volunteers from the Coldstream and Scots Guards. G and Y Patrols routinely operated from Siwa. (IWM, HU 016614)

The first campaign in the Fezzan, February–March 1942

The Free French forces did not understand the experience of the LRDG, though partly this was for political reasons. The Free French needed to have an active campaign of their own with which they could demonstrate their own vitality unsupported by the British. Though politically valid, these priorities proved impractical in the field. By the winter of 1941/42 desert-raiding forces were no longer a surprise to the Italians, whose defences in the Fezzan had been improved since the previous winter. Intended to start simultaneously with Eighth Army's Operation *Crusader*, the Free French raid in the Fezzan was overly ambitious. A large number of units were collected, including Geoffroy's Patrouille A (which was to raid in the area Hon–Brak–Sebha), Détachement Guillebon (bound to the area Tmessa–Zuila–Um el Araneb) and Détachement Hous which, along with Groupement d'attaque Dio and Patrouille D, was to

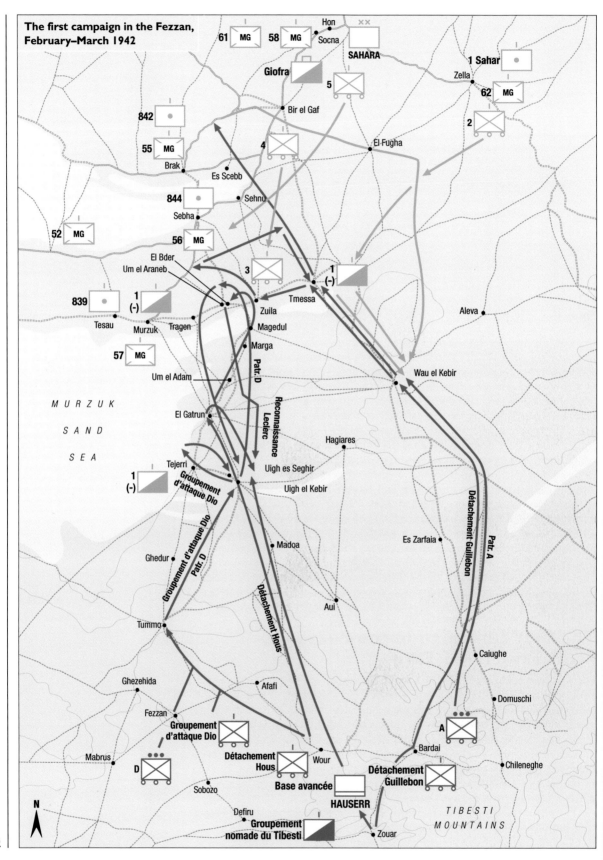

The first campaign in the Fezzan,
February–March 1942

61 MG 58 MG Hon
Socna
×× SAHARA
Giofra 5
1 Sahar Zella
62 MG
2
842
55 MG
Brak
Es Scebb
Bir el Gaf
4
El-Fugha
844
Sehnu
Sebha
52 MG
56 MG
El Bder
Um el Araneb
3
1 (-)
Tmessa
Aleva
839
1 (-)
Tesau
Murzuk
Tragen
Zuila
Magedul
Marga
57 MG
Um el Adam
Patr. D
Reconnaissance Leclerc
Wau el Kebir
M U R Z U K
S A N D
S E A
El Gatrun
Hagiares
Tejerri
Uigh es Seghir
1 (-)
Groupement d'attaque Dio
Uigh el Kebir
Es Zarfaia
Détachement Guillebon
Patr. A
Ghedur
Madoa
Groupement d'attaque Dio
Patr. D
Aui
Tummo
Caiughe
Détachement Hous
Ghezehida
Afafi
Domuschi
Fezzan
A
Groupement d'attaque Dio
Wour
Bardai
Mabrus
Détachement Hous
Chileneghe
Base avancée
Détachement Guillebon
D
HAUSERR
Sobozo
TIBESTI MOUNTAINS
Defiru
Groupement nomade du Tibesti
Zouar

N

seize the Wau el Kebir–Tejerri area before moving further north up to Um el Araneb, while Sarazac's Groupement nomade du Tibesti was to protect the lines of communications and Hauserr's Base avancée. The weak point of the plan was that it was neither a major attack nor a series of coordinated raids, but rather an odd mixture of both. The units engaged were too weak to sustain any major combat, particularly against Italian forts, and they were scattered over a wide area, far from their own supply bases. For example, Groupement Dio was required to cover some 1,600km, Patrouille A as much as 3,800km. It was also practically impossible to group the forces together to meet any serious challenge, particularly once surprise had been lost.

By mid-February Free French forces had grouped in the area of Zouar and Wour and on the 17th the infiltration phase began. Ten days later Patrouille D and the Détachement Hous had reached the Uigh el Kebir, where a patrol of the 1ª Italian Compagnia Meharisti was captured. The following morning Free French forces had no problem in overwhelming and capturing the small Italian garrison at Gatrun, but an Italian reconnaissance plane discovered

Vehicles derived from the TL37 artillery tractor, like this armed version, had good off-road mobility and were heavily armed. (Filippo Cappellano – AUSSME)

Logistical support for the Colonne Leclerc. Camels bring supplies to a forward base during the French raid towards Kufra. (Memorial Leclerc)

their presence and they had to withdraw. On the very same day Groupement Dio seized Tejerri by a *coup de main*, overwhelming another detachment from 1ª Compagnia Meharisti. On 1 March Patrouille D attacked Um el Araneb, but the fierce resistance of the Italian garrison compelled the French French to withdraw. In the meantime, Détachement Guillebon had reached Tmessa, which was attacked the same night; once more the *Meharisti* detachment collapsed and the French forces destroyed all the Italian military installations. On the night of 2/3 March Patrouille A, which had reached the Brak area, ambushed and captured an Italian convoy carrying aviation fuel. The Free French had reached all their objectives without major problems. But the Italians were unwilling to lose their positions and reacted strongly. On 1 March the 3ª and 4ª Compagnie Sahariane moved to the threatened area; by the 2nd the 3ª Compagnia Sahariana was at Um el Araneb while the 4ª Compagnia Sahariana met and engaged Patrouille A halfway between Hun and Sebha. The same night Détachement Guillebon attempted to attack the Italian garrison at Zuila but without success. On 3 March, the 3ª Compagnia Sahariana attacked Patrouille D in the Um el Araneb area, while two other *Sahariana* companies (one of which, the 5ª, lacked motor vehicles) were activated. The French had lost both the element of surprise and the advantage of numbers.

Leclerc's attempt to regroup his scattered forces in the Um el Araneb area failed, and only elements from Détachement Hous, Groupement Dio and Patrouille D remained in the area while both Patrouille A and Détachement Guillebon marched their way back following the same route they had taken before. The former achieved the last success of the first Fezzan campaign on 7 March, when the Italian garrison at Wau el Kebir was attacked. However, at Um el Araneb the 3ª and 4ª Compagnie Sahariane – supported by Italian aircraft – soon forced the remaining Free French forces into a general withdrawl. By 14 March 1942 all the Free French forces were at Zouar, thus ending their first campaign in the Fezzan. Casualty figures are difficult to work out for sure, but Italian sources report some 40 Free French dead and 19 vehicles destroyed at the cost of three Italian dead, seven wounded and 47 missing. French sources report this campaign as a success, but very little had been achieved.

The LRDG/SAS partnership, March–May 1942

The Fezzan campaign only confirmed what the LRDG had already learned in February 1941: desert-raiding forces, owing to their structure and organization, were not suited to attacking enemy units and positions deep in their rear areas. By October 1941 the patrols of the LRDG had been reorganized and greatly

The LRDG/SAS partnership, March–May 1942

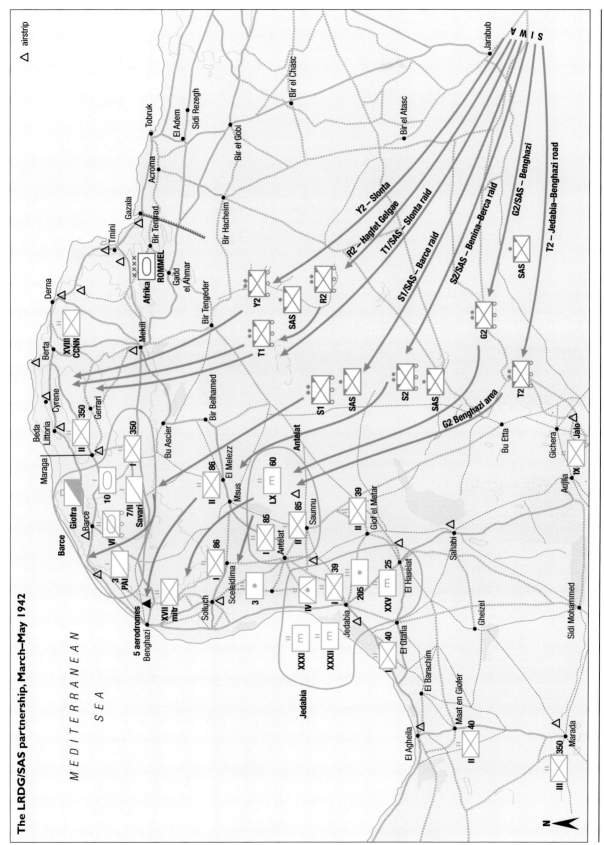

△ airstrip

Place names visible on map: Jarabub, Bir el Chasc, Bir el Atasc, Tobruk, El Adem, Sidi Rezegh, Bir el Gobi, Acroma, Bir el Hacheim, Gazala, Tmini, Bir Temrad, Derna, Berta, Cyrene, Beda Littoria, Maraga, Mekili, Bir Tengeder, Bir Belhamed, Bir Hacheim, Gerrari, Bu Ascier, El Melezz, Msus, Giofra, Barce, Benghazi, Solluch, Sceleidima, Antelat, Saunnu, Giof el Matar, Bu Etta, Gichera, Aujila, Jalo, Sahabi, El Haselat, Gheizel, Sidi Mohammed, Jedabia, El Gtafia, El Barachim, Maat en Giofer, El Agheila, Marada

Gadd el Ahmar, Afrika, ROMMEL, 5 aerodromes

Raid labels:
Y2 – Slonta
R2 – Hagfet Gelgae
T1/SAS – Slonta raid
S1/SAS – Barce raid
S2/SAS – Benina–Berca raid
G2/SAS – Benghazi
T2 – Jedabia–Benghazi road
G2 Benghazi area

MEDITERRANEAN SEA

S I W A

N

Unit markers: Y2, SAS, R2, T1, S1, SAS, S2, SAS, G2, Y2, XVIII CCNN, 350, 350, 86, LX 60, E 85, II 85, I 85, 86, II 39, 39, 205, E 25, XXV, 40, I, E XXXI, E XXXII, IV, 3, XVII mitr, 3 PAI, VI, 7/II Savari, 10, II 40, III 350

reduced in strength, now numbering only five or six vehicles rather than 12. This way they could escape the enemy's attention and reconnaissance more easily, even though their combat strength had been further reduced. In theory this should have left them with only reconnaissance missions to perform; however, their experience gained through dropping of agents in enemy territory led to a new form of 'taxi driving'. On 17 November 1941 R1 Patrol left Siwa in order to collect 55 members of Captain David Stirling's Special Air Service, who had been dropped at Bir Temrad (south-west of Gazala) during the night of 16/17 November to attack the enemy airstrips at Tmimi and Gazala. The LRDG patrol reached the rendezvous point two days later to find that the SAS men had scattered over a wide area when dropped and had not only failed to complete the mission, but only 21 out of 55 made it back to the rendezvous. This bitter experience taught valuable lessons and it was clear that instead of being dropped from the air, the SAS needed to be ferried to their targets by patrols of the LRDG.

The first raid using this new form of cooperation took place between 8 and 16 December 1941, when S1 Patrol dropped Captain Stirling, Lieutenant Mayne and 11 men of the SAS close to the Sirte airstrip. Although Stirling's mission was a failure because there were no aircraft there, Mayne's was not and he succeeded in destroying 24 aircraft and a petrol dump at Tamet airstrip. Both parties were successfully collected by S1 Patrol and eventually brought back to Jalo. LRDG and SAS cooperation increased after Rommel's second drive into Cyrenaica. On 9 March 1942 the Eighth Army HQ issued detailed instructions to the LRDG, Middle East Commando and SAS to take every effort 'to weaken the enemy's main forces, to cause him to disperse his efforts and, in particular, to lower his morale'. This goal was to be attained through

An SAS team and their heavily armed jeeps. The combined skills and experience of the LRDG and SAS proved extremely effective and gave the Allied forces an invaluable asset for threatening the Axis rear areas. (IWM, E 21338)

intensive sabotage of enemy's lines of communication, airstrips and bases in order both to compel the Axis forces to detach units for security duties and to damage and destroy as many facilities as possible. The joint LRDG/SAS campaign started only a week later. S2 Patrol was the first to leave with an SAS and Folboat party bound for Benina and Berca on 15 March, followed a day later by S1 Patrol headed for Barce airfield. The first raid was only partly successful, but the SAS assault on Berca airfield on 20/21 March ended with the destruction of 15 aircraft. Another SAS/Folboat raid against Benghazi and Benina on 25/26 March ended without any serious damage to shipping and only five aircraft destroyed at Benina airfield. On 16 March T1 Patrol undertook a joint mission with SAS men against Slonta, which was the target of another raid on 31 March, this time carried out by Commandos along with Y2 Patrol. On 5 April R2 Patrol undertook a mission to the Hagfet Gelgaf (in the Jebel Akhdar) to pick up a seven-man party of the SAS while dropping Arab agents in the area; when the area was reached the patrol found some other Eighth Army personnel and another Libyan Arab Force officer that it brought back to Siwa along with the SAS men.

What is surprising at first sight is the relative slackness of the Axis forces in the area, especially if compared to the – likewise relatively – energetic reaction of the Italian Sahara defence forces earlier the same year against the Free French forces. There was no shortage of Axis combat forces in the area: between Derna and El Agheila there were elements from two divisions plus other army, corps and garrison troops to give a total of 20 battalions and three artillery regiments, including tanks, armoured cars and Libyan mounted troops. Notwithstanding these resources, the Italians did not manage to cause any serious threats to the LRDG/SAS raids, though there were occasional clashes. It was clear that units shaped for conventional warfare were not able to respond to the new challenge. The lack of *Compagnie Sahariane* (all stationed in the Fezzan) was a key factor in explaining the ineffective Axis reaction to LRDG/SAS activity

The LRDG missions were so successful that on 23 April 1942 Eighth Army HQ issued new instructions further increasing the role of the unit. C Squadron of Middle East Commando was put under its command and joint LRDG/SAS missions continued in the following months.

On 9 May 1942 S2 Patrol and Middle East Commando made a raid on the Jebel Akhdar, though it proved unsuccessful due to enemy activity. A raid by G2 Patrol and the SAS against Benghazi was also unsuccessful: though they succeeded in entering the town, they were not able to carry out any of the intended sabotage against enemy shipping. On 26/27 May Rommel launched his offensive against the Gazala Line that eventually stopped some two months later at El Alamein. This led to a whole range of new tasks for the LRDG and the SAS.

The big raids, September 1942

As opposed to their European history, the story of Commando operations in North Africa before the summer 1942 is one of disappointment. Of the four Middle East Commandos formed in spring 1941, two, A and D Battalions, were practically wiped out during the battle for Crete, losing 800 out of 1,200 men. B Battalion was deployed at Tobruk during the siege and subsequently disbanded, while C Battalion was deployed in Syria against Vichy French troops. All in all, they performed very few of the Commando operations that they had been trained for, and those that they did take on resulted in little success: their first raid on Bardia on 19 April 1941 and their assault against what was believed to be Rommel's HQ at Beda Littoria on 17/18 November both ended in failure. Between late November 1941 and August 1942 no more seaborne Commando raids were carried out against Axis-held positions in North Africa, while the growing success of the LRDG/SAS operations showed how the latter were better suited to carrying out sabotage raids behind enemy lines.

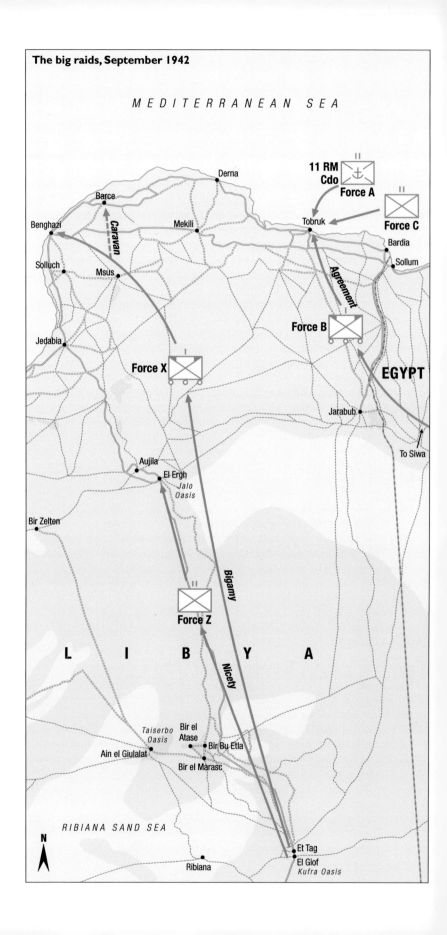

The big raids, September 1942

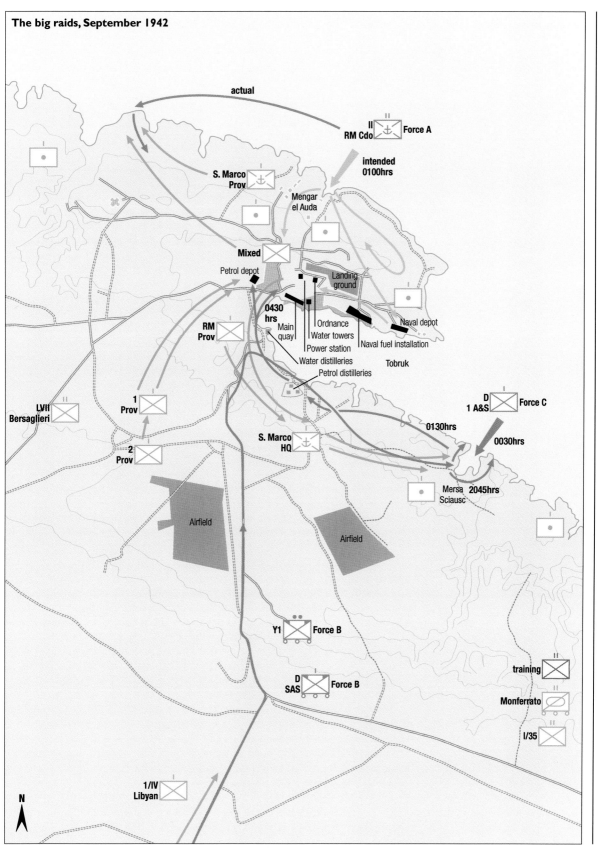

The big raids, September 1942

actual

II RM Cdo — Force A

intended 0100hrs

S. Marco Prov

Mengar el Auda

Mixed

Petrol depot

Landing ground

0430 hrs

Main quay

Ordnance

Water towers

Power station

Water distilleries

Petrol distilleries

Naval depot

Naval fuel installation

Tobruk

RM Prov

D 1 A&S — Force C

0130hrs

0030hrs

LVII Bersaglieri

1 Prov

2 Prov

S. Marco HQ

Mersa Sciausc 2045hrs

Airfield

Airfield

Y1 — Force B

D SAS — Force B

training

Monferrato

I/35

1/IV Libyan

N

69

Table 17: Operation *Agreement*											
	Enlisted						**40mm**	**50mm**	**76mm**			
Officers	**men**	**Rifles**	**MPs**	**LMGs**	**HMGs**	**guns**	**mortars**	**mortars**	**jeeps**	**lorries**	**W/T**
Force A	24	396	330	40	27	4	0	0	6	0	0	4
Force B	8	192	140	24	13	2	2	0	0	11	19	1
Force C	11	281	258	14	9	4	0	3	0	0	0	1
Totals	43	869	728	78	49	10	2	3	6	11	19	6

In summer 1942, Rommel's advance into Egypt changed the focus of special forces' operations in North Africa. The new threat caused by the presence of Axis forces so close to Alexandria switched Middle East HQ's attention towards a large-scale deployment of the special forces at their disposal, one that could really make a difference from a strategic point of view. The idea, which had been under development ever since the withdrawal from Cyrenaica, was quite simple: since Rommel's supply lines were overstretched, sabotaging one of the main harbour facilities at his disposal would cause the Axis forces to face a massive logistical problem. As fuel was the scarcest item for the Axis in North Africa, it was decided to mount an assault on the fuel storage facilities at Tobruk and Benghazi.

The assumption was made that Tobruk and Benghazi would be garrisoned by low-grade Italian forces and, although not all the special forces approved of the idea, between the end of August and early September a plan was eventually worked out. The main stroke was to be delivered at Tobruk (Operation *Agreement*) and was aimed at destroying the harbour and main depots in the area. This operation was to be covered by two further raids aimed at Benghazi (Operation *Bigamy*), where Stirling's SAS was to destroy the local harbour and storage facilities, as well as raiding the air bases at Benina and Barce (Operation *Caravan*). Operation *Nicety* was designed to seize the Jalo Oasis, and was intended to support the withdrawal of those raiding forces that were not going to be re-embarked. Operation *Agreement* was the most ambitious part of the plan. It involved a joint LRDG/SAS party known as Force B seizing an inlet east of Tobruk (Mersa Sciausc) where, later the same night, seaborne troops carried aboard MTBs were to be landed (Force C). At the same time as this force moved against Tobruk and its harbour, destroying enemy positions in their, a Royal Marine Commando Battalion (Force A, landing from the destroyers HMS *Sikh* and *Zulu*) was to land further north of Tobruk, at Mersa Mreira, seize the coastal batteries located in the Tobruk peninsula and enter the town. The raiding forces were to remain at Tobruk for a full day, with part of the force leaving on the afternoon of D+1 and another part, hopefully including a sizeable proportion of the 16,000 British prisoners supposedly held at Tobruk – were to move westwards disrupting the enemy's lines of communication before re-embarking later that night. The LRDG/SAS party was to retreat through the desert to Jalo.

Force B, including D Squadron SAS and Y1 Patrol of the LRDG, set out from Cairo on 22 August and, after a short halt at Kufra, left for Tobruk on 5 September, which they reached on the 13th. Led by three captured lorries with German-speaking agents aboard, the SAS party successfully passed through the enemy defences and reached Mersa Sciausc, which was captured without major problems. After this point almost everything went wrong. The heavy air bombardment alerted the local Italian forces without inflicting heavy casualties on them. Most of the Force C MTBs failed to see the guiding lights set by SAS men and only two succeeded in landing their men, who were welcomed by heavy fire from Italian positions. Force A experienced similar problems and improvised landing craft had problems in finding the right beach. After a delay of around two hours, about 70 Royal Marine Commandos were landed at Mengar el Auda, some two miles to the west of the intended landing beach, where they were subdued by defensive fire. Though not strongly garrisoned, Tobruk was defended by a marine battalion of the San Marco Regiment, a first-rate unit. These troops, along with a mixture of Italian Army, *Carabinieri*, PAI, Navy, Libyan and German soldiers reacted with unexpected speed and aggression, and soon trapped the SAS and Force C at Mersa Sciausc. meanwhile another provisional company of the San Marco Regiment along with a mixed company from Tobruk attacked Force A at Mengar el Auda. Worst of all, two Italian armed barges prevented the other British vessels from reaching the coast and the Italian coastal batteries heavily shelled HMS *Sikh* and *Zulu*. At sunrise, German and Italian aircraft relentlessly attacked the two damaged destroyers, eventually sinking them; they also destroyed the AA cruiser HMS *Coventry* and three MTBs. Overwhelmed by the number and firepower of the defenders, the men of Force A and Force C, plus part of the SAS force, were compelled to surrender. The total losses incurred during Operation *Agreement* included 280 naval personnel, 300 Royal Marines and 160 soldiers killed, wounded or captured (the Italians reported 30 dead, 515 prisoners plus other 59 wounded prisoners). Amongst those killed was the commander of Force B, Lieutenant-Colonel J. E. Haselden, on whose body the Italians found the plans for Operation *Agreement*, as well as for Operations *Bigamy*, *Nicety* and *Caravan*. Axis losses were extremely light: 16 dead (one German) and 50 wounded (seven Germans).

Operation *Bigamy* was a failure as well, though not as costly as Tobruk. Force X fell behind its timetable and was discovered by enemy reconnaissance. The attempt to attack Benghazi was, in practice, never carried out. Following a clash at a roadblock and with the sun rising, Colonel Stirling decided to withdraw. The Force Z attack on Jalo suffered a similar fate: as the Axis possessed details

Operation *Agreement*: three LRDG jeeps on the edge of the Sand Sea during the operation by T and G Patrols to raid the Axis airfield and fuel dump at Barce. Major Jake Easonsmith, leader of the patrol, is behind the wheel of the nearest jeep. (IWM, HU 016666)

of the British plans, the garrison had been alerted and strengthened and easily repelled the first attack carried out during the night of 15/16 September. Eventually, Force Z was ordered to withdraw on the 19th, before an Italian column could reach the oasis. Only the subsidiary Operation *Caravan* at Barce achieved a level of success, though still at a high cost. T1 and G1 Patrols reached Barce during the night of 13 September. Once more Italian reconnaissance spotted the approaching vehicles, but the local defenders (which included the 3ª PAI company, a *Carabinieri* company, the 2ª company of XVII MG Battalion and the 10ª Compagnia Carri Leggeri) set up a poor defence. The Italian commander could not believe that the British party would use vehicles to carry out the attack and assumed that they would try to approach on foot. The LRDG force, led by an experienced commander in Major John Easonsmith, easily overwhelmed a road block south of Barce and headed at full speed toward the airstrip and the village. T1 Patrol attacked the former, while the latter was attacked by G1 Patrol They easily overwhelmed the Italian sentries and roadblocks leading to the airstrip and for about one hour the New Zealand patrol was free to destroy aircraft. Eventually the patrol withdrew because it was running low on ammunitions; all in all it destroyed 16 Italian aircraft (mostly bombers) and damaged seven more. However, the Italians aggressively pursued the retreating patrols, mainly using aircraft, and caused severe losses to the LRDG force. Only three LRDG vehicles out of 17 made their way back, losing 13 missing men and ten wounded.

The raids in Egypt, July–August 1942

Owing to its peculiar characteristics, the Western Desert was not suitable for raids or Commando-style operations on a large scale. Add to that the fact that a large number of the troops taking part in the 'big raids' were inexperienced, as well as lacking suitable weapons and equipment, and their failure is not hard to understand. However, in the previous months the LRDG carried out business as usual – small missions behind enemy lines. With the Axis forces at El Alamein and the threat of a breakthrough to Alexandria looming, the LRDG's missions were aimed to directly hit behind enemy lines. On 1 July 1942 G1 and Y2 Patrols were assigned an operational area stretching from the Alamein Line to some 130km to the west; their duty was to act like modern-day pirates, attacking enemy convoys and destroying lorries carrying petrol and water.

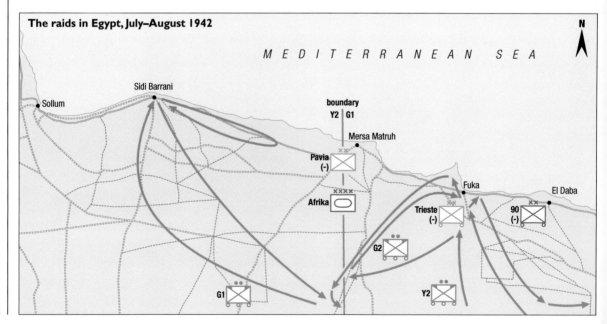

The raids in Egypt, July–August 1942

Von Almaszy's mission to Egypt

The difference between the activity of the LRDG and the failure of the Axis forces to develop any real desert-raiding unit is striking. The failure on the Italian side can be explained by the slow reactions and sloppiness of their highest echelon of military leaders; however, it is harder to understand the German attitude. The story of Operation *Salaam* and of the man that made it possible shed a little more light on the German approach to special forces. The Hungarian Count Ladislas 'Lazlo' Edouard de Almaszy (known to the Germans as von Almaszy) had been, along with Bagnold, Clayton, Shaw and Prendergast, a member of the select club of desert explorers in the 1930s. Recruited by the German intelligence organization, the Abwehr, and made a major in the Luftwaffe, he was involved in two Abwehr failures in Egypt. The first involved an attempt to pick up the chief-of-staff of the Egyptian Army, el Masri

Von Almaszy's base camp in Tripoli, just before he set off on the long trip to the Nile to drop off two spies. (Carlo Pecchi)

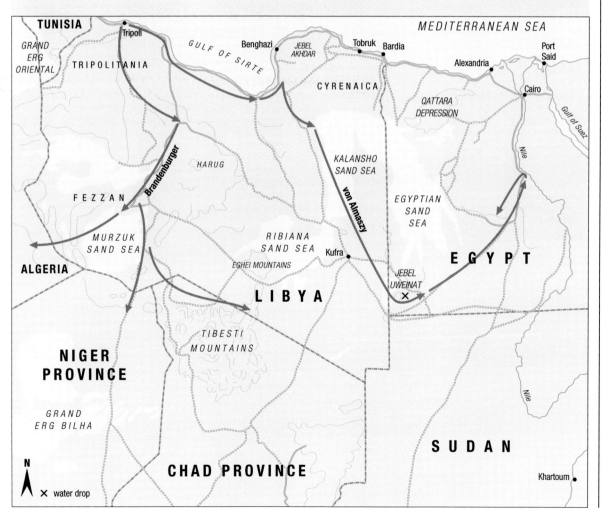

Pasha, and the second was an aborted attempt to drop two German agents by air. Eventually, von Almaszy was authorized to raise a small party to drop two German agents close to Cairo. This was to be the start of Operation *Condor*, a Germans attempt to set up an intelligence ring deep in enemy territory.

In February 1942, the Sonderkommando Almaszy (Special Command Almaszy) was formed in Germany made up of personnel from the Brandenburg Regiment and equipped with six British captured vehicles: three Ford C11ADF 4 x 2 cars and three Ford F8 4 x 2 1.5-ton lorries, which were sent to Tripoli via Naples by April. Von Almaszy and his men (nine Brandenburgers plus the two agents) had reached Tripoli well before to acclimatize themselves and to prepare the desert equipment. This included sun compasses and the same gear used by LRDG patrols to cross the desert, plus some powerful wireless sets and special rations prepared by the Luftwaffe. Von Almaszy, his men and the two spies wore German uniforms to avoid any trouble in case of capture, and their vehicles bore German insignia in order to disguise the secret nature of the mission. On 29 April the party moved from Tripoli to the Jalo Oasis, then in Axis hands, where Rommel took the opportunity of meeting them. Soon afterwards, the party moved to the deep desert heading to the south-east across the Kalansho Sand Sea. The high temperatures, around 50°C, and the need to travel at full speed across the sand dunes to avoid becoming stuck proved too much for two members of the party, who fell ill. Von Almaszy had to return to Jalo, rest for about ten days and reconsider his plan. To avoid crossing the arduous Kalansho Sand Sea, he decided to take

Men of von Almaszy's party recover cached supplies. Cooperation with the Luftwaffe proved a key factor in von Almaszy's success. (Carlo Pecchi)

a more southerly route that brought the party first to the south-east of Kufra, then close to the Libya–Egypt–Sudan border. Such a change of route meant that more fuel, water and food were needed. A solution was found with the help of the Luftwaffe, whose planes dropped extra supplies (mainly water and gasoline) at pre-determined points along the way. Finally, by mid-May 1942 the party moved again from Jalo heading this time south-south-east.

This route proved much less arduous and the Egyptian border was reached without further difficulties. The party slipped past the Kufra garrison and crossed the border heading towards an old water dump von Almaszy had established in 1937. Although the maps supplied by the Italians proved to be useless, von Almaszy's skill and experience enabled the mission to continue. Eventually the party reached the Gilf Kebir Pass, where it took the desert track leading east toward the

Nile. The Kharga Oasis was reached the day after, and there von Almaszy used his knowledge of Arabic and local customs to convince the Egyptian garrison that he and his men were the spearhead of a British column on its way back to Cairo. A couple of days later, two weeks after setting off from Jalo, the party finally reached its objective, the village of Asyut some 500km south of Cairo. The two spies changed into civilian clothes and walked into the town; von Almaszy and the Brandenburgers started their way back to Jalo. Operation *Salaam* had been a success, though Operation *Condor* proved a failure as the two spies were arrested a few months later having supplied no worthwhile intelligence. British intelligence turned the captured cipher (codenamed 'Rebecca', after the novel by Daphne du Maurier) to their own advantage and began sending false information to Rommel's headquarters, though this was discounted as the code had already been compromised.

Von Almaszy subsequently disappeared from the desert, playing no further role in the development of German raiding forces. Eventually, a unit was formed using the Brandenburgers, and its three patrols were used to perform raids in depth into French-held territory.

Von Almaszy's vehicles negotiating a difficult passage in the desert. Von Almaszy's skill, determination and attitude could have made him an effective leader of a German counterpart to the LRDG, but the Hungarian nobleman's talents were wasted.
(Carlo Pecchi)

An Italian motorized column. The first and last vehicles are AS37 trucks. Axis truck convoys were high-priority targets for LRDG and SAS patrols. (Filippo Cappellano – AUSSME)

Y2 Patrol passed the Alamein Line north of the Qattara Depression, and was later ordered to make contact with G1 Patrol and an SAS detachment at Qaret Turtura, some 150km south of Mersa Matruh. However, G1 Patrol failed to cross the line and it was not until 6 July that the two patrols joined up, along with G2 Patrol. Put under the command of Major Stirling, the three patrols carried out a series of raids on the Axis lines of communication. On 8 July an SAS party carried by G2 Patrol attacked a landing ground close to Fuka, while Y2 and G1 Patrols were unable to find suitable targets. On the night of 10/11 July, Y2 Patrol was spotted and attacked by enemy aircraft while preparing to attack a landing ground near Fuka, Lieutenant Gurdon was lost in the process. From this point on the LRDG patrols were busy for the rest of the month carrying agents of the G(R), the Interservice Liaison Department and 'Popski's Private Army' across the lines. On 26 July an SAS party led by T1 Patrol successfully attacked an air strip near Mersa Matruh, and some 30 German aircraft were destroyed. Enemy aircraft and truck-borne infantry attacked the patrol the following day, though without loss. These activities soon became a great source of concern for the Axis forces, though little if anything could be done to prevent them.

The Axis LoC in Egypt was already overstretched, especially as the lack of troops made it impossible to garrison the area properly. In summer 1942 the only Axis combat units deployed west of the Alamein Line were elements from the German 90.Afrika Division and elements of the Italian 'Trieste' and 'Pavia' Divisions. Security duties in the area were therefore neglected, and aircraft represented the main instrument to search for, and where possible attack, enemy patrols. The LRDG patrols were rarely spotted and even more rarely attacked.

Command, control, communications and intelligence (C3I)

A motorcycle squad of the Polizia dell'Africa Italiana (PAI) receives instructions from an officer atop a SPA AB41 armoured car. The officer is standing on the back of the armoured car, where a Breda 38 machine gun was positioned. The motorcyclists are armed with the 9mm Beretta 38 submachine gun. The one on the right carries a gas mask pouch slung across his chest. (Piero Crociani)

Command

Command represents a key feature that clearly distinguished the British, and to a certain extent the Free French, attitude toward the use of special forces in the desert from that displayed by the Italians and the Germans. The latter never developed a single, centralized command system to oversee the development and the employment of the forces used in the Sahara to counter LRDG and SAS raids behind their lines. The Italian structure of command was decentralized following a geographical pattern that saw the Comando del Sahara Libico as being distinct from the Tripolitania and Cyrenaica

commands. In spite of the LRDG's increased activity, a single command structure capable of dealing with such a highly mobile raiding force was never created, and single local commanders had to deal with the threat as best they could with locally available resources. These resources were rarely able to meet the threat but individual commanders, such as General Piatti Dal Pozzo of the Comando del Sahara Libico, were able to make a difference through their individual skills and abilities.

Personalities played a major influence in the war that was fought behind the main front line. Without a D'Ornano or a Leclerc, the Free French forces would not have been able to develop their skills and capabilities to the point where they could effectively launch successful campaigns. This is an area where the Germans lacked individual leadership. With the notable exception of Count von Almaszy, whose skills and capabilities were underemployed, their special

The LRDG's command and control in the field

From June 1940, when the first patrols were formed, general control of LRPU (later LRDG) operations was officially entrusted to the Deputy Director Military Intelligence (DDMI), Middle East Command, Cairo, and this was the status quo (excluding some short periods) until the end of North African campaign. However, control in the field was limited by the same factors that had pushed Maj. Bagnold to adopt a 'loose' organization structure for the LRDG patrols. Although orders were directly issued from Cairo HQ – who also collected all the data gathered during the missions – the LRDG enjoyed a great deal of operative autonomy, which was only partially reduced by its subordination to Eighth Army's HQ. During this period, one or more patrols were temporarily transferred from the LRDG to other units (Brigadier Reid's 'Force E', or Brigadier Marriott's 'Marriott Force') to assist on particular tasks, but these were always temporary attachments. To a certain extent, it could be said that the nature of LRDG operations did not allow them to be encased in the tight framework of a rigid control system. The 'double hat solution' was the one most often adopted, with patrols answering to LRDG HQ for their 'core duties' and to another HQs (usually the HQ of a unit to which patrols were detached) for auxiliary activities.

LRDG organization, based on semi-independent patrols, proved especially suited to this solution, largely adopted during the second part of its operative life. Single patrols – as autonomous and self-reliant forces – could generally be detached without seriously affecting either their short- to medium-term capabilities, or the wider organization of the LRDG; at the same time, they could also be attached to the new units without

the need to change their chains of command, operative structures, or logistic establishments. Wireless communications ensured constant contact between patrols, LRDG HQ and other units' HQs, as well as between LRDG HQ, Cairo HQ and Eighth Army HQ, allowing orders and reports to flow in a number of directions, and in a relatively short time, as happened during the first phase of the British offensive in autumn 1941, when the 'low profile' of LRDG patrols was shifted to a more aggressive attitude following the German counterattack of 20–24 November.

Broadly speaking, the LRDG control system also seems, hence, to adapt to a more general pattern, on one side typical of all contemporary armies, on the other paying a special attention to the very peculiar nature of desert warfare, where the main assumptions of the 'empty battlefield model' are often taken to their extreme. Loose chains of command, the 'double hat system', and patrol detachment were, in this perspective, the way in which both LRDG and the higher commands tried to cope with the inherent difficulties of a modern, highly mobile war in a particularly hostile environment. The flourishing of autonomous or semi-autonomous units, both in the British Army and among its Italian and German counterparts, is in itself a good proof of the soundness of these solutions, and the wide deployment of these kinds of unit in other theatres of war – both during and after World War II – seems to move in the same direction. However, it is worth noting how it was specifically to fit the desert's special features that these tools had been invented, and that their transfer to different contexts has often proved troublesome, as attested by the experience of the LRDG after its shift from North Africa to the Aegean and Italy from 1943 onwards.

forces lacked the distinct leadership that might have led to them threatening the Allied forces in a meaningful manner. For the British, one might argue that there were rather too many personalities involved. Ralph Bagnold's skills and capabilities, along with General Wavell's personal interest in the subject, proved essential to the development of a desert-raiding force. That the LRDG not only survived, but even increased its size and importance, after Bagnold relinquished command in favour of Guy Prendergast is particularly noteworthy though not surprising, since both belonged to the pre-war 'club' of desert travellers. Moreover, Bagnold's appointment to Middle East Command HQ also helped the LRDG press its claims at the highest levels in Cairo. However, the proliferation of special forces units, 'private armies', in the Western Desert often led to command and control issues. Following the failure of September 1942's 'big raids' General Alexander empowered a single staff department at HQ Middle East Command – the General Staff Operations (Raiding Forces) – with the task of coordinating all special operations in the area. This resolved any disputes between Prendergast and Stirling and established a special forces' central command in North Africa.

Control

The wideness of the operational area, its rough physical characteristics, shortcomings in wireless communications and the sheer length of the missions all ensured that central control was somewhat lacking. That was true for both the British and Free French raiding forces, and also for the Italian defenders. The latter's complete lack of reaction when faced with the first LRDG raid in the Fezzan and the Free French seizure of Kufra in the winter of 1940/41 clearly suggests that there were severe problems in local command and control. General Piatti Dal Pozzo overcame many of these shortcomings as is shown by the reaction during the first Free French Fezzan campaign in spring 1941. This same campaign illustrates the importance of control for raiding forces: Leclerc's troops were working to a prearranged plan and, facing unexpected developments, proved unable to adapt to the changing situation. However, Leclerc was at least able to rely on a group of handpicked, skilled officers capable of leading their units even in difficult circumstances. The British special forces also had the advantage of a skilled officer corps, while the Germans and Italians were particularly unfortunate, especially the latter, whose colonial officers were in many cases completely unfit to face the demanding challenges posed by modern, well-equipped special forces. The case of the Kufra garrison, which surrendered without firing a single shot, is particularly extreme.

The LRDG relied on a highly effective command and control structure that enabled it to face and overcome unexpected situations. From its inception, the kind of missions entrusted to LRDG imposed the need to develop a flexible as

A German column of the Sonderkommando Dora moving in the desert. This special unit trained intensively in the deep Sahara. (Memorial Leclerc)

possible command structure. Communications amongst patrols, and between them and HQ, were often difficult due to the technical limits of the No. 11 wireless set. Personal skills thus played a large role in the selection of LRDG officers. The first batch of officers was almost entirely composed of Maj. Bagnold's personal friends who had participated in his travels in the Western Desert. Self-reliance, autonomy and experience in desert navigation were key factors in the selection process, while professional backgrounds varied greatly. Bagnold himself came from the Royal Service Corps and Maj. Prendergast from the Royal Tank Regiment. Of the three first LRPU patrol commanders, Capt. Mitford came from the RTR, Capt. Clayton from the General List, and Capt. Steele from the NZEF.

A second feature stemming from the special character of LRDG missions was the streamlined organization of the group. The command structure of LRDG always remained remarkably flat, although the frequent attachment and detachment of units complicated the hierarchical chain somewhat. Until December 1940, the HQ establishment was extremely slim, with practically no other level of command between it and the individual patrols. Only from spring 1941, with the formation of three new patrols and the dramatic increase in the establishment of the LRDG, was a new HQ set up to coordinate the group support units, while subordinate HQs were formally introduced at both squadron and patrol level. However, the actual number of staff employed did not really grow. The actual rise in HQ personnel was mainly due to the absorption of men from the subordinated sections, while squadron HQs comprised just one officer, one WO, one NCO and eight other ranks for a total of 11 men. By the end of the period in question, the evolution of the LRDG favoured the emergence of a more traditional chain of command and the development of tight coordination with other units, which affected the traditional autonomy of the patrol commanders. However, until the end of its presence in North Africa, the LRDG largely conserved its 'informal' structure and acted as a reference point for the organization of other British special forces units like the Middle East Commandos and the 1st SAS Regiment.

Communications

The ability to stay constantly in touch with their HQ, and with the HQs at Cairo, was essential for LRDG patrols, whose missions lasted a long time deep behind enemy lines. Through the HQs, the patrols could be informed about the movements of both enemy and Allied troops; their mission targets could be updated or even changed; and arrangements could be made to drop supplies at given points or to collect wounded personnel. Moreover, LRDG HQ could be informed of the progress of individual patrols that enabled them to plan further operations. However, communications in the desert were problematic at best. The only feasible mean of communicating over such long distances was by radio, which could be listened in to by the enemy.

The LRDG's radio communication also involved several technical problems: the most widely used radio set was the No. 11 wireless set, a portable, general-purpose, low-power transceiver dating back to 1938. Its normal range was only about 30km and it had to be rigged for long-range use, which involved the use of a 2m whip antenna or a Wyndom aerial slung between two 5m-high wooden poles. So radio could be used only in secure areas and after some preparation. Personnel also had to be selected and particularly trained and, as Morse code was largely used, the first LRDG radio operators were selected from cavalry units of the New Zealand division and from the Royal Corps of Signals, though some experience with either the Merchant Marine or Marconi Company long-range code procedures was also required. Following the expansion of the LRDG, radio operators were either selected from or trained by the Irregular Wireless Operators School (IWOS),

Two men of an LRDG patrol, dressed in greatcoats, make use of available cover while on a road watch. These missions gave the British HQ a lot of useful information about Axis movements and activities. (IWM, E 012434)

run by the intelligence section of the Middle East Forces' HQ. This was also important as operators needed to be trained in the use of codes.

The Italians also realized that radio communications were essential not only to maintain contact with their garrisons and outposts in the desert, but also to achieve a better control of their mobile fighting units. This was not easy to achieve as in 1940 the Italian communications system in the Fezzan consisted of around 40 fixed and mobile radio stations spread all over an area of 1,000,000km^2. In 1942 these were manned by the Compagnia Mista Genio del Sahara Libico (Libyan Sahara Mixed Engineers Company), which had a strength of eight officers and 200 other ranks. Most of the radio sets were heavy and cumbersome and it was not until late 1942 that the Italians equipped two lorries for use as mobile, long-range communications centres. Several small radio sets were built using spare parts and scraps, and these were used to equip the newly formed *Compagnie Sahariane*. Their main shortcomings were the limited range and the lack of trained personnel to effectively use and maintain them. Details are scarce, but it also appears that these problems influenced the Italian monitoring of LRDG radio signals, which were only sporadically detected.

Intelligence

As most of the activity of the LRDG was in the field of intelligence, this particular field has great relevance. The need for good reconnaissance and intelligence gathering lay behind the decision to create the first Long Range

Desert Patrol. Working in cooperation with the Director of Military Intelligence Staff of GHQ Middle East Forces and taking advantage of the Libyan Senussi tribe's traditional animosity toward the Italians, Captain J. R. Easonsmith, a newcomer to the LRDG, successfully succeeded in getting a number of Arab agents behind enemy lines, dropping them in the Jebel Akhdar region close to Tobruk. There a network of agents was established, to be eventually led by the Belgian-born son of a Russian émigré, Major Vladimir 'Popski' Peniakoff, who was later to lead LRDG's No. 1 Demolition Squadron. Thanks to his close relationships with the Libyan Arab Force, the British-sponsored Senussi militia, Peniakoff built up an organization active not only in sabotage, but also in intelligence gathering. Arab agents, supported by British liaison officers and wireless operators, were dropped by LRDG patrols in the Jebel Akhdar, where they were left for up to five months.

British intelligence was not always successful when dealing with special forces operations. The failure of the raid against Rommel's presumed HQ at Beda Littoria is a clear example of faulty intelligence, and this kind of experience was not uncommon, with the most serious case taking place during the raids in Cyrenaica in September 1942.

One particular intelligence-gathering mission at which the LRDG excelled was 'road watching'. These missions were generally carried well behind the front line with the sole purpose of 'counting' the number and type of enemy vehicles moving along the main – and only – road in Libya, the Via Balbia. From early 1941, the main intelligence source for the British was the deciphering of the German high-level radio traffic, the source known as 'Ultra'. However, as British commanders soon learned, this source could be misleading because of Rommel's tendency to paint to his superiors in Berlin a gloomier picture than it actually was. The road watching missions of the LRDG were essential in confirming the Ultra information, or filling in gaps that it left.

What is surprising looking at the 'other side of the hill' is the fact that, in spite of accurate and timely intelligence about the LRDG and other British special forces in the Western Desert, the Axis forces failed to make good use of it. Although the Italians were completely caught by surprise in winter 1940/41 by the LRDG's first mission, the capture of Capt. Clayton and several valuable documents at Jebel Sherif enabled them to gain an accurate picture of the LRDG's organization and mission, to the extent that the Italians started to send bogus messages compelling LRDG patrols to switch codes. However, Capt. Clayton apparently supplied false information about LRDG targets during his interrogation, highlighting the oasis of Jalo and the Fezzan. It is therefore not so surprising after all that the Italians and Germans were almost completely unprepared to counter LRDG missions in Cyrenaica and Tripolitania. Italian intelligence about the Free French forces in Chad proved particularly useful in the spring of 1942, when the Italian *Compagnie Sahariana* effectively drove them from the Fezzan.

Weapons and equipment

Weapons

In almost every case, the weapons used by special forces in the desert were the standard weapons issued to combat units in the Western Desert. Like any other combat formation in desert conditions, the special forces faced a number of problems with these weapons, principally due to the sand and dust that meant that they needed to be constantly cleaned and maintained. Special forces also needed a wide variety of weaponry to make up for their shortage in numbers. As the LRDG found during their first raid in the Fezzan, firepower was essential for small, mobile units. They also needed their weapons to be reliable and sturdy enough to cope with the difficult conditions of the desert.

The personal weapons of the LRDG were Ordnance Branch standard issue and included a large variety of rifles (mainly SMLE Mk III, and Lee-Enfield No. 4 Mk I), pistols and revolvers. Automatic weapons (Thompson machine guns, both 1928 and M1 versions) were issued on a large scale to provide patrols with better firepower. Bombs, landmines and grenades, generally the No. 36 Mills grenade, were also widespread. Italian and German weapons were generally issued for special missions and returned on the completion of the mission. However, captured weapons were increasingly retained by the LRDG, both as souvenirs and persoanl weapons. Side arms, such as the Italian Beretta M34 automatic pistol and German P08 Luger and P38 Walther, and German machine pistols such as the MP38 and MP40 were the most coveted, although the German MG34 and MG42, and Italian Breda 37 and 38 machine guns, were widely used as well.

Italian and Libyan troops in the Fezzan had very few automatic weapons. The standard weapon was the 6.5mm Carcano Model 91 (musket and rifle versions). The Italian machine pistol, the 9mm MAB Beretta Mod. 38/42, was

A 20mm Breda M35 dual-purpose gun in an emplacement. It was very effective against both aircraft and ground targets, and was highly appreciated by both sides. From spring 1942 the Breda 20/65 equipped the *Compagnie Libice da Posizione* and the *Compagnie Sahariane*. (Piero Crociani)

only used to equip special formations like the paratroopers, PAI patrols and Arditi. Heavy weapons were even more rare, except for the 6.5mm light MG Breda Mod. 30 that was flimsy and unreliable. The Libyan *Compagnie Mitraglieri da Posizione* were equipped with the heavy, tripod-mounted and water-cooled World War I-vintage 8mm Schwarzlose 07/12 or the equally outdated 6.5mm Fiat Mod. 14. Local garrison units appropriated the weapons from the Aviazione Sahariana planes. These were the 7.7mm and 12.7mm Breda SAFAT and proved to be extremely effective weapons when mounted on tripods or trucks. The only anti-tank weapon available to Italian troops in the Sahara, at least until spring 1942, was the Swiss-made 20mm Solothurn anti-tank rifle, capable of firing a 337g round at 832m per second. There were almost no heavy weapons or light artillery available to Italian troops in the Sahara.

In comparison, the LRDG was lavishly equipped. Their trucks carried six to eight pivots that could be used as gun mountings, though normally only two or three of them were used. At different times, weapons mounted on these pivots consisted of Vickers .303in. liquid-cooled (Vickers Maxim), double-barrelled Vickers 'K', single-barrelled Vickers 'KO', and Vickers .50-cal. machine guns; Browning AN M2 .30-cal. and .50-cal. machine guns; Lewis Mk. I .303in. guns; Boys AT rifles; 37mm Bofors AT guns; and captured Breda 20mm dual-purpose (AA/AT) guns. Some LRDG trucks also carried OML 2in. mortars. Some of these weapons (the Lewis gun, Boys AT rifle and Vickers Maxim) were rather old fashioned, but they were robust enough to endure the desert conditions and simple to use. Others (Vickers 'K' and 'KO' machine guns, the Browning AN M2 .30-cal.) were chosen because they were readily available as they were surplus to RAF requirements.

The high level of firepower of the LRDG patrols enabled them to effectively disengage from contact with the enemy and also to deal with desert outposts

A German intelligence report showing 'English sabotage material'. The drawing at top right shows three different ignition systems (time fuse by corrosion, bolt blow fuse and ignition cord burning at the speed of 1cm per second), the capsule containing the detonating mercury, the fuse and the explosive bag. Shown on the left are details of the bolt blow fuse and, below, the detonating capsule. The use of two different ignition systems on the same device was commonplace. (National Archives and Records Administration, USA)

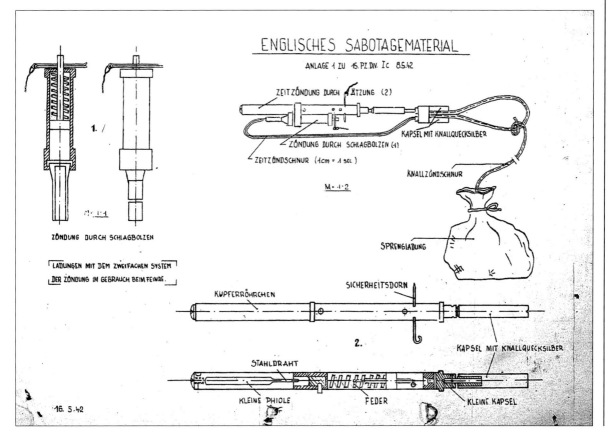

ENGLISCHES SABOTAGEMATERIAL

ANLAGE 1 ZU 15.PZ.DIV. Ic 8.5.42

ZEITZÜNDUNG DURCH ÄTZUNG (2)

KAPSEL MIT KNALLQUECKSILBER

ZÜNDUNG DURCH SCHLAGBOLZEN (1)

ZEITZÜNDSCHNUR (1cm = 1 sec.)

KNALLZÜNDSCHNUR

M. 1:2

ZÜNDUNG DURCH SCHLAGBOLZEN

SPRENGLADUNG

LADUNGEN MIT DEM ZWEIFACHEN SYSTEM DER ZÜNDUNG IM GEBRAUCH BEIM FEINDE.

KUPFERRÖHRCHEN

SICHERHEITSDORN

2.

KAPSEL MIT KNALLQUECKSILBER

STAHLDRAHT

KLEINE PHIOLE   FEDER   KLEINE KAPSEL

16.5.42

and convoys. Despite the potent weaponry, the main assets of the LRDG were stealth and mobility. Patrols were generally ordered to avoid contact with the enemy as much as possible in order not to compromise their missions. This largely explains why, soon after its creation, the cumbersome LRDG Heavy Section was quickly disbanded.

After the reorganization of spring 1942 the Italian troops in the Sahara gained an improved allocation of heavy weapons. The *Compagnie Libice da Posizione* and *Compagnie Sahariane* were equipped with the 81mm Model 81 mortar, which fired a 2.4kg projectile to a range of 3,100m, the 8mm Fiat Mod. 35 tripod-mounted heavy machine gun and the 20mm Breda Mod. 35 AA/AT gun, which was extremely effective. The spring of 1941 also saw the arrival of several Italian Army artillery units in the Sahara, which greatly increased the firepower of local garrisons. Apart from the 77mm 77/28 infantry gun that equipped the Italian Army units, a 1ª Batteria Sahariana was also formed equipped with the 75/27 Mod. 911, which had an effective range of 8,300m.

Vehicles and equipment

In a war of mobility vehicles play a vital role. To perform its duties, the LRDG – and to a certain extent the Free French forces – adopted a wide range of vehicles from different sources: the Egyptian Army, private purchase and the official channels of the British Army. These vehicles can be grouped under four main categories: (1) pilot vehicles (Ford 01 and 15-cwt Chevrolet 1311X3, later US-made four-wheel drive Willys jeeps and 8-cwt CMP Fords), which were lighter and faster than standard patrol cars and better suited for scouting and vanguard actions; (2) patrol vehicles (Chevrolet WB, Ford F30 15-cwt, and 30-cwt Chevrolet 1533X2), which made up the main body of the unit; (3) Heavy Section vehicles (6-ton Ford Marmon-Herringtons, 10-ton Whites, Mack NR9 N44, Ford F60 CMP and some captured Italian 6-ton Lancia 3RO and Fiat AS37s), which were generally used to carry the supplies; (4) special vehicles, which were adapted for special duties such as medical supply trucks, wireless trucks, light artillery trucks (nicknamed 'scorpion's tails') and medical staff trucks, also used as field ambulances. All the LRDG vehicles were especially fitted to operate in a desert environment. Their most noteworthy character was the condenser cooling system, which prevented the water in the radiator from boiling over in the high temperatures. The condenser was a brainchild of Bagnold and it dated from the late 1920s. The sun compass was another piece of equipment issued as standard to LRDG vehicles. Bagnold's sun compass was a major departure from the more traditional model that was widely adopted by both the British Army and RAF, as it showed the true bearing at any time. The standard pattern needed resetting

The most powerful version of the AS42 Sahariana was armed with a 47/32 gun and two 8mm machine guns. The 47/32 gun had AT and fire-support capabilities. (Filippo Cappellano – AUSSME)

every time the vehicle changed its course, which was troublesome and time consuming. Errors due to the different sun position on different days and at different hours were corrected by monitoring the BBC time signal through a Philips receiver carried on the wireless truck. Star fixes and magnetic compasses were also used to check the data gathered from the sun compass. To avoid potentially fatal navigation mistakes, one of the main tasks of LRDG navigators was to take a daily star fix of their actual position, check it with the one calculated through sun compasses and speedometers, and amend any eventual discrepancy. Commonly used equipment mounted on LRDG lorries included sand tyres (16in. low-pressure tyres); 'unsticking equipment', which included pioneer tools, sand channels and sand mats; jerrycans (the much-coveted German containers that were more reliable than the standard British ones) and flimsies. The load carried by LRDG vehicles also included wireless sets and receivers, cold storage boxes, stretchers and other equipment. To keep the weight of the trucks as low as possible (a 30-cwt truck could be loaded with 1.5 tons of supply and weapons, and a 15-cwt with about 0.5 tons), to reduce petrol consumption (a 30-cwt Chevrolet 1533X2 could manage some 12 miles to the gallon) and improve mobility they were completely unarmoured.

This specialized equipment enabled the LRDG to retain a decisive edge over their opponents, who in general had much poorer vehicles. It is interesting to note that the Germans were never capable of developing or producing a vehicle that was really suited to the desert. The vehicles of the Sonderkommando Dora

The light and agile American Willys jeep proved a perfect vehicle for raiding missions. The LRDG and SAS soon modified jeeps with specific equipment and heavy weaponry. (IWM, E 21338)

The Autocarro Sahariano AS37 was in service with the Italian motorized units in charge of the defence of the Fezzan. Their overall performance was good, which made them a much-sought-after prey for Allied units. (Filippo Cappellano – AUSSME)

were the standard ones used to equip the Afrika Korps and proved dramatically unsuitable for both the terrain and for the long distances the patrols were required to cover. The only vehicle that proved satisfactory was the Kübelwagen, due to its light weight, modified air intakes and filters and the widespread use of over-sized low-pressure aircraft tyres, 'borrowed' from Junkers Ju 88 bombers. However, the effects of sand and dust (in spite of the special filters) greatly reduced the long-range capabilities of these vehicles. Although the Kubelwagen could manage between 50,000 and 70,000km in Europe, it could do only 12,000–14,000km in North Africa. Other vehicles performed even worse: the Horch and Kfz 17 cars suffered greatly from suspension weaknesses, as did the Opel 'Blitz' truck. The Germans also never developed any navigation device comparable to those used by the LRDG, relying on aircraft compasses and captured British ones. Generally speaking, the Germans and Italians regarded the vehicles used by the British as superior and used captured vehicles whenever possible. That does not mean, however, that all the vehicles used by Axis forces were completely unsuitable for the desert and some of the Italian vehicles proved successful. The Fiat/SPA AS37 was a light, 3-ton lorry based on the TL37 artillery tractor and possessed good cross-country capabilities. Thanks to its large, over-sized, tyres and to the four driving and steering wheels, it could easily negotiate terrains otherwise impenetrable to other, heavier vehicles. With a gun (usually a Breda 20mm or a 47/32 AT gun) mounted on its flat bed, or just used as a troop carrier, it was largely used by the *Compagnie Sahariane* companies, though its mechanical reliability could not be compared to that of the vehicles commonly used by the LRDG and it was prone to suffer major breakdowns after around 5,000km.

The Italians eventually managed to produce the only vehicle of the era specifically conceived for desert raiding, the AS42 Sahariana. Following the LRDG's first raid into the Fezzan the Italian Army Staff issued a specification for a fast, well-armed, long-range vehicle specifically destined for use in the Sahara. The result was a 4.5-ton vehicle, based on the chassis of the AB40/41 armoured car, with a 100hp engine capable of a maximum road speed of

84km/h and a range of 300km, which could be increased further by carrying additional fuel in canisters (the vehicle had external racks for 24 jerrycans, 20 of which were used to carry fuel). The SPA-Viberti AS42 Sahariana could carry a crew of six plus a wide array of weapons. The main armament included a 20mm Solothurn AT rifle or a 20mm Breda gun, with in some cases a 47/32 AT gun. Secondary armament included up to three 8mm Breda 37 machine guns, one of which could be dismounted to be used outside the vehicle. Four-wheel drive, large tyres and sturdy chassis gave this vehicle an adequate cross-country capability, which made it perfectly suitable for use in the desert. Production difficulties delayed its delivery and the first eight Sahariana did not arrive at Hon till November 1942, followed soon by two other vehicles, and the crews came from the 10a Arditi, a unit specifically formed following the example of the British special forces. Soon after their arrival, these vehicles withdrew to Tunisia, where they were joined by other Sahariana manned by the 10ª Arditi and were employed as conventional units. Some 300 Sahariana were built in all. It is also worth mentioning that some of these fought on the Eastern Front as part of the 10ª Arditi which joined the German 2.Fallschirmjäger Division in September 1943 following the Italian surrender. The only mission the Sahariana never accomplished was the one it had been built for: carrying out raiding missions in the desert.

Two Ford trucks used by the Sonderkommando led by Count von Almaszy during Operation *Salaam*. The use of captured vehicles was due not only to a desire to deceive the enemy, but also to the German lack of suitable vehicles. (Carlo Pecchi)

Lessons learned

Assessing today the lessons learned from the experiences of the 'desert raiders' during the campaign in the Western Desert is somewhat problematic. The main purpose behind Bagnold's creation of a desert-raiding force was the setting up of a force able to strike deeply behind enemy lines with the twofold aim of disrupting the lines of communication through sabotage and the gathering of useful intelligence. As such, the concept proved extremely successful; not long after the creation of the Long Range Desert Group in North Africa, this concept was put into effect almost all over Axis-occupied Europe, particularly after the conclusion of the war in North Africa. After 1943 Allied – and British in particular – special forces and intelligence bodies began to harass the Germans in most of the countries they occupied: France, Italy (especially after the Italian surrender and the beginning of the Italian campaign in September 1943), the Low Countries, Yugoslavia and Greece. This programme of harrassment was almost always undertaken in conjunction with local resistance movements and partisans who were becoming increasingly active against the German occupiers, and the methods used were completely different from those pioneered by the LRDG in 1940–42.

Air drops and amphibious landings were used to smuggle troops across, or just behind, the enemy lines instead of motor vehicles; this was the approach developed by David Stirling (though it did not work particulary well in the desert) and these concurrent developments might lead one to assume that Bagnold's development of the LRDG was nothing more than a variation of other developments taking place in the realm of irregular warfare. However, that would just be a short-sighted view that does not take into account the peculiarities of the desert raiders.

A more accurate analysis of what lies behind the 'strike deeply behind enemy lines' concept is revealing. First of all, depth has a particular value here; in both cases, in the Western Desert and in occupied Europe, targets were located in areas well behind the front line, out of reach of any striking force other than the air forces. In many cases, both in the Western Desert and in German-occupied Europe, air forces might have damaged the enemy lines of communication faster than special forces did and to a greater extent. This then raises the question: why were special forces largely used when air forces might

Two AS42 Sahariana on patrol. These vehicles were designed from the outset to be used for desert raiding. The Italians followed the example of the LRDG and SAS and set up a unit with similar capabilities (the 10ª Arditi) equipped with specialized vehicles. (Filippo Cappellano – AUSSME)

have done their job? Two main aspects of the answer can be summed up as intelligence gathering and harassment. Both of these roles were carried out by ground-based special forces units in a very different way from air forces. Particularly with regard to the harassmenbt of the lines of communication, the effects of ground-based units such as the LRDG were deeper and longer lasting; while it was possible to fight against enemy air activity simply with anti-aircraft artillery and air defence squadrons, special forces had to be fought by troops permanently garrisoning any perceived target alongside other, more mobile troops capable of striking back and destroying the raiders. In both cases, the enemy lines of communication were threatened and its resources stretched trying to defend them both from the air and from the land. Since the matter has been long debated, though not studied in detail (at least, concerning special and raiding forces), it is hard to say how really effective they were during World War II.

Axis reaction to the threat posed by the LRDG in the Western Desert may offer an answer. After the first LRDG operations, the Italians greatly increased the number of troops garrisoning the Sahara (from 2,900 in October 1940 to 5,800 in November 1942), thus draining resources that could have been employed in the front line. And, together with the Germans, they tried to build their own desert-raiding force. It is a matter of fact that, just shortly after Bagnold's idea had turned into a reality, it was imitated by all other forces fighting the war in the desert, though results were often incomparable. But it must always be remembered that the Bagnold's brainchild, perfectly suited for the local environment, practically ended there as the subsequent lacklustre performances of the LRDG in the Aegean in 1943 and in Italy in 1944 well demonstrate. It's clear that in a different environment like continental Europe, each specific skill that had made LRDG's men unique and valuable in the Western Desert lost its relevance.

Interaction with the environment

So, one may be tempted to reach the conclusion that the desert raiders experience only had a limited, local value. But this would be a major mistake because the principal lesson (not always properly learned) remained that the LRDG was an extremely effective raiding force mainly because it was closely bonded to its natural environment, the Sahara Desert. Knowledge and specific skills made its men and capabilities unique.

For contemporary special forces this means that the local factor must always be taken into account as a key factor. Training, careful selection of men and hi-tech weapons alone cannot be enough to assure success. Local environment always means a lot and is of utmost importance: this is the real heritage of Bagnold's approach. He put the natural environment first, shaping accordingly means, organization and tactics. He also knew that the decisive edge over the adversary lay in the deeper knowledge of the specific environment and not in better weapons or more powerful means.

If this view is correct, we should be able to recognize some traces of this approach in the modern special forces and when we look, for example, at the special forces in the Vietnam war, at their failures and successes and the way they changed and tried to evolve, we can see that in the background the key factor was their ability to interact with the local environment. This interaction was what the desert raiders mastered best, the core idea that justified their existence and the most effective lesson they left to any force committed to the unconventional dimension of warfare.

Chronology

1940

10 June	Italy declares war to France and the United Kingdom
25 June	France surrenders to Germany and Italy
3 August	Italian attack against British Somaliland, Berbera is seized on the 19th
26 August	Chad is taken over by De Gaulle's Free French forces
5 September	First LRDP mission in Libya which ends at the end of the month, the patrol reaches Chad
13–16 September	Italian offensive against Sidi Barrani
8–10 November	Major Bagnold is at Fort Lamy (Chad) to make contact with the Free French
9 November	The new organizational scheme for the LRDG is approved by the War Office
23 November	First LRDG mission starts (W Patrol, back to Cairo on 6 December)
2 December	Leclerc takes over command of Free French forces in Chad
9–10 December	Start of British offensive (Western Desert Force) against the Italian positions at Sidi Barrani that becomes Operation *Compass*
23 December	The Groupe nomade du Tibesti, led by Captain Sarazac, starts its raid in the Fezzan; it will raid Tegerhi on 13 January 1941
27 December	Second LRDG operation (T and G patrols, ended 9 February 1941)

1941

5 January	Bardia, on the Egypt–Libya border, falls to the 6th Australian Division
11 January	LRDG and Free French forces capture Murzuk
19 January	The British offensive against Italian East Africa starts at Kassala in Eritrea
22 January	Tobruk is captured by the Western Desert Force
23 January	Free French forces led by Leclerc moves against Kufra Oasis, which surrenders on 1 March
30 January	Derna is captured by the Western Desert Force
3 February–27 March	The Italians are defeated at the battle of Keren and withdraw from Eritrea, Massaua is seized by British forces on 1 April 1941
5/6 February	Italian forces are destroyed at Beda Fomm ending Operation *Compass*. Benghazi is seized by the British forces
9 February	The Western Desert Force reaches El Agheila
12 February	Erwin Rommel and the vanguard of the Afrika Korps reaches Tripoli
25 February	British forces advancing from Kenya seize Mogadishu in Italian Somaliland
24 March	German and Italian forces seize El Agheila. On the same day the LRDG's G Patrol sets out for a reconnaissance mission to Cyrenaica, marking the beginning of A Squadron's activity in the region which lasts until July
2 April	Rommel's drive into Cyrenaica starts6 April 1941 – The Italians are defeated at Addis Ababa, Ethiopia's capital city
9 April	The LRDG sets off towards Kufra Oasis, which is reached on the 25th
10–11 April	The first German attack against Austrialian forces at Tobruk ends in a failure
19/20 April	A battalion of Layforce (formerly No. 7 Commando) raids Bardia
30 April–2 May	Rommel's second assault on Tobruk, after its failure the fortress is besieged
2 May	Iraqi forces attack the British garrisons at Basra and Habbaniyah
3–19 May	Amba Alagi, the last Italian-held position in Italian East Africa, falls to the British
10 May	British forces from Transjordan enter Iraq starting the seizure of the country. Fallujah is occupied on the 19th and by the end of the month an armistice is reached at Baghdad
12 May	The 'Tiger' convoy arrives at Cairo, bringing armour for the Western Desert Force
15 May	Operation *Brevity*, the British attack at Halfaya Pass and Fort Capuzzo
7 June	LRDG's A Squadron is reorganized and G, Y and H Patrols are formed
9 June	Free French and British forces enter Syria from the Lebanon

15 June	Start of Operation *Battleaxe*, the British offensive against Halfaya Pass and Fort Capuzzo. It ends on June 17 without success
1 August	Lieutenant-Colonel Bagnold is promoted to fullcColonel and leaves the LRDG, Lieutenant-Colonel Prendergast takes charge
24 September	HQ British Eighth Army is formed under command of Lieutenant General Sir Alan Cunningham, the LRDG forms part of his command
30 October	The LRDG's patrols are split in two following a reorganization
17/18 November	Commando raid led by Lieutenant-Colonel Geoffrey Keyes against Rommel's presumed HQ at Beda Littoria
17/18 November	L Detachment SAS under command of Major Stirling raids against the enemy airfields at Gazala and Tmim
18-19 November	Start of Operation *Crusader*, the British offensive to relieve Tobruk
16-17 December	German and Italian forces withdraw from eastern Cyrenaica and are back at El Agheila by 6 January 1942

1942

21 January	Start of Rommel's second drive through Cyrenaica, which ends on 5/6 February at the Gazala Line
17 February	Free French forces start their first campaign in the Fezzan
26 May	Rommel's assault against the Gazala Line
10–11 June	German and Italian forces under Rommel's command break through the defences of the Gazala Line and head for Tobruk
20 June	Tobruk is seized by Axis forces, two days later Rommel decides to advance into Egypt
26–28 June	Battle of Mersa Matruh, the Eighth Army withdraws to the Alamein Line
1–4 July	Battle of First Alamein, Rommel's advance is halted
7–8 July	Eighth Army's counterattack at Tel el Eisa
14–15 July	First battle of Ruwesait Ridge
21–22 July	Second battle of Ruwesait Ridge
30/31 August	Rommel's offensive against the Alamein Line, the ensuing battle of Alam Halfa lasts until 4 September
13/14 September	Operations *Bigamy* (Benghazi), *Agreement* (Tobruk), *Nicety* (Jalo) and *Caravan* (Barce)
23/24 October	Led by Montgomery the Eighth Army attacks the Axis position at Alamein, the offensive lasts until 1 November
2 November	Montgomery's final offensive at Alamein, Operation *Supercharge*
4 November	Rommel orders a retreat from the Alamein Line
8 November	Allied forces land in Morocco and Algeria
10–11 November	German forces establish a bridgehead in Tunisia; Axis forces under Rommel's command withdraw from the Egypt–Libya border
16 December	Free French forces start their second campaign in the Fezzan

1943

4–6 January	Free French and LRDG forces seize the villages of Um el Araneb and Gatrun
6–9 January	The Italians retreat from the Fezzan, on 8-13 January the Free French forces seize Hon
23 January	Tripoli is seized by the Eighth Army; 7th Armoured Division links with the Free French forces coming from the Fezzan
4 February	The last Italian and German forces cross the Tunisian border – end of the Western Desert campaign

Bibliography

Carell, Paul, *Die Wüstenfüchse. Mit Rommel in Afrika* (Frankfurt: Ullstein, 1989)

Corbonnois, Didier, and Godec, Alain, *L'Odyssée de la Colonne Leclerc: Les Français Libres au Combat sur le Front du Tchad, 1940–43* (Paris: Histoire et Collection, 2003)

Cowles, Virginia, *The Phantom Major: The Story of David Stirling and the SAS Regiment* (London: Collins, 1958)

Crichton-Stuart, Michael, *G Patrol* (London: Kimber, 1958)

Degli Esposti, Fabio and Pecchi, Carlo, 'Tedeschi sul Nilo', *Storia Militare* No. 30, March 1996

Gordon, John W., *The Other Desert War. British Special Forces in North Africa, 1940–1943* (New York: Greenwood, 1987)

Harrison, D., *These Men are Dangerous: The SAS at War* (London: Blandford Press, 1988)

Hoe, Alan, *David Stirling: The Authorised Biography of the Creator of the SAS* (London: Little Brown and Company, 1992)

James, Malcolm, *Born of the Desert: With the SAS in North Africa* (London: Greenhill Books, 2001)

Kay, R. L., *Long Range Desert Group in Libya, 1940–41* (Wellington, NZ: War History Branch – Department of Internal Affairs, 1949)

Kay, R. L., *Long Range Desert Group in the Mediterranean* (Wellington, NZ: War History Branch – Department of Internal Affairs, 1950)

Kemp, Anthony, *SAS at War: 1941–45* (London: John Murray, 1991)

Kennedy Shaw, W. B., *Long Range Desert Group* (London: Greenhill Books, 2000)

Kurowski, Franz, *Deutsche Kommandotrupps 1939–1945. »Brandenburger« und Abwehr im weltweitem Einsatz* (Stuttgart: Motorbuch, 2004)

Lloyd Owen D. L., *The Desert My Dwelling Place* (London: Cassell, 1957)

Lloyd Owen D. L., *History of the Long Range Desert Group: Providence Their Guide* (Barnsley: Pen and Sword, 2000)

Lytton, Noel A., *The Desert and the Green* (London: MacDonald, 1957)

Messenger, Charles, *Middle East Commandos* (London: Kimber, 1988)

Neillands, Robin. *Raiders: The Army Commandos, 1940–1946* (London: Weidenfeld, 1989)

Peniakoff, Vladimir, *Popski's Private Army* (London: Cape, 1950)

Playfair, I. S. O. et al., *History of the Second World War: The Mediterranean and Middle East, vol 1: The Early Successes against Italy, to May 1941* (London: HMSO, 1954)

Playfair, I. S. O. et al. *History of the Second World War: The Mediterranean and Middle East, vol 3: British Fortunes Reach Their Lowest Ebb* (London: HMSO, 1960)

Spaeter, Helmuth, *Die Brandenburger. Eine deutsche Kommandotruppe zbV 800* (Düsseldorf: Dissberger, 1991)

Timpson, Alaistair, and Gibson-Watt, Andrew, *In Rommel's Backyard: Behind the Lines with the LRDG* (Barnsley: Pen and Sword, 2000)

Smith, Peter C., *Massacre at Tobruk* (London: Kimber, 1987)

Swinson, Arthur, *The Raiders: Desert Strike Force* (New York: Ballantine, 1968)

Vincent, Jean Noël, *Les Forces Française Libres en Afrique, 1940–1943* (Château de Vincennes : Ministère de la Défense, État-Major de l'Armée de Terre – Service Historique, 1983)

Wynter, H.W., *Special Forces in the Desert War, 1940–1943* (London: Keeper of the Public Records, 2002)

Glossary

Abbreviations (as used on tables)

AA	Anti-aircraft		Mot	*Motorisiert* (motorized)
AC	*Anti-chars* (anti-tank)		NCO	Non-commissioned officer
Art	Artillery		Offs	Officers
AT	Anti-tank		OR	Other ranks
Batt	*Batteria* (battery)		PAI	Polizia Africa Italiana (Italian Africa Police)
Cie	*Compagnie* (company)		PdC	Poste de commandement
CO	Commanding officer		Pl	*Peloton* (platoon)
Cp	*Compagnia* (company)		POL	Petrol, oil, lubricants
DC	*Découverte et de combat* (reconnaissance and combat company)		PPA	Popski's Private Army
			R&F	Ranks and file
Fla	German Army Flak (AA)		RA	Royal Artillery
Fusil	*Fusiliers*		Rep	Repairs
FV	*Fusiliers voltigeurs*		Rgt	Regiment
GNB	Groupement nomade du Borkou		RTST	Régiment de tirailleurs sénégalais du Tchad
GNE	Groupe nomade de l'Ennedi		SAS	Special Air Service
GNT	Groupe nomade du Tibesti		SdC	*Section de commandement* (command post)
Gpo	*Gruppo* (group)		SdMitr	*Section de mitralleuses* (MG section)
HMG	Heavy machine gun		SdMort	*Section de mortiers* (mortars section)
ILRS	Indian Long Range Squadron		Sec	Section
Kp	*Kompanie* (company)		Sion	Section
LoC	Line of communication		Sq, Sqn	Squadron
LMG	Light machine gun		SS	Special Service
LRDG	Long Range Desert Group		Tp, Tps	Troop, troops
MG	Machine gun		WO	Warrant Officer
Mitr	*Mitralleuses* (machine-gunners)			

Place names

Italian	English	French	Arab
Agedabia	Jedabia/Ajedabia		Ajdabiya
Augila	Aujila	Zuilla	
Bisciara	Bishara		
Ciad	Chad	Tchad	
Cirenaica	Cyrenaica		
Cufra	Kufra	Koufra	Al Kufra
Gatrun	Gatrun	Gatroun	Al Qatrun
Gebel Akdar	Jebel Akhdar		Jebel el Akhdar

Place names *continued*

Italian	English	French	Arab
Gebel Scerif	Jebel Sherif		
Gialo	Jalo	Djalo	Jalu
Giarabub	Jarabub		
Hun	Hon	Hon	Hun
Mechili	Mekili		
Murzuch / Murzuk	Murzuk	Mourzuk	Murzuq
Sebha	Sebha	Sebha	Sabha
Siwa	Siwa		
Tagrifet			
Tazerbo	Taiserbo	Tazerbo	Tazirbu
Tegheri	Tejerri	Tedjere	
Tragen	Tragen	Tragnen	
Um el Araneb	Um el Araneb	Umm el Araneb	
Uao / Uau el Kebir	Wau el Kebir	Ouaou el Kebir	
Uweinat	Uweinat	Auenat	
Zella	Zella	Zilla	
Zuar		Zouar	

Ranks

Italian	English	French	German
Sottotenente	1st Lieutenant	Sous-lieutenant	Leutnant
Tenente	Lieutenant	Lieutenant	Oberleutnant
Capitano	Captain	Capitaine	Hauptmann
Maggiore	Major	Commandant	Major
Tenente-Colonnello	Lieutenant-Colonel	Lieutenant-Colonel	Oberstleutnant
Colonnello	Colonel	Colonel	Oberst

Index

References to illustrations are shown in **bold**.

aircraft
  Caproni Ca309 Ghibli **52**
  Savoia Marchetti SM82 Marsupiale **9**
  Supermarine Spitfire 48
  Waco biplane 20
Alexander, Gen. Harold 78

Bagnold, Col. Ralph A. 7–8, 10, 11, 13, 14, 15, 19, 53
  and command, control and communications 77, 78, 79
  and equipment 84
  and lessons learned 88, 89
Balbo, Marshal Italo 27
Barce airfield 67, 70, **71**, 72
Bedouin tribesmen 14
  see also Senussi tribe
Benghazi 67, 70, 71
Benina airfield 67, 70
Bir Hacheim 47
British forces 9
  see also Indian Army, Long Range Desert Squadron
  Commandos, Middle East 23, 24, 67
  Duke of Westminster's No. 2 Armoured Motor Squadron 9
  Hussars, 11th 57, 60
  Layforce 20, 22
  Long Range Desert Group see Long Range Desert Group
  Long Range Desert Patrol (LRDP) 14–15, 50, 80–81
    organization 15–16, **16**
  Long Range Patrol Units (LRPU) 14
  New Zealanders 14, **14**–15, **16**, 72
  'Popski's Private Army' 13, 24, 75, 81
  Royal Marine Commandos 70–71
  Special Air Services Regiment, 1st (formerly Special Air Squadron; L Detachment, Special Air Service) 12, 13, 22, **66**, 75
    D Squadron 70
    establishment (Sept. 1942) **25**
    Folboat Section 24
    Free French Squadron 24
    joint operations with LRDG 22, 23, 24, 64, **65**, 66–67, 70, 71
    M Detachment 24
  special forces 7–8
  unit organization 14–26
    see also Long Range Desert Group: organization
Bu Ngem fort **4**

camel-mounted troops see Italian forces: Compagnie Meharisti; Libyan forces, *Meharisti* units
Canaris, Adm. 48
Caputo, Tenente 52
Chad 38–39, 48, 81
Clayton, Capt. Patrick A. 14, 15, 50, 52, 79, 81
Colonna, Capitano 57
Colonne Leclerc (formerly RTST) **56**
  bataillon de marche No. 3: 41
  Compagnie portée du Cameroun 44
  compagnies de découverte et de combat (DC, reconnaissance and combat companies) 39, 41
  Détachement Guillebon 41, 61, 64
  Détachement Hous 41, 61, 63, 64

Groupement D 44
Groupement d'attaque Dio 41, 61, 63, 64
Groupement G 44
Groupement M 44
logistical support **64**
organization 39, 41, 44
  Jan.–Mar. 1941 **39**
  Feb.–Mar. 1942 **40**, 41
  Dec. 1942–Jan. 1943 **42**, **43**, 44
patrouilles 41
combat mission 6–8
command 76–78
communications 79–80
compasses 84–85
control 78–79
Coventry, HMS 71
Crichton-Stuart, Capt. M. D. D. 16
Cyrenaica 28, 30, **34**, 46, 57, 66, 81
  reconnaissance in 57, **59**, 60–61

D'Ornano, Lt. Col. 38, 50, 52, 53
de Gaulle, Gen. Charles 38
doctrine 9–12

Easonsmith, Maj. John R. 'Jake' **71**, 72, 81
Egypt, LRDG raids in 72, 72, **73**, 75
Egypt, von Almaszy's mission to **73**, 73–74, **74**, **87**
Eichler, Obstlt. Walter 48
environment, interaction with 89
equipment 84–85

Fezzan, the 6, 18, **27**, 37, **38**, 38, 41, 44, 48, 57, 78, 81
  LRDG in (27 Dec. 1940–9 Feb. 1941) 50, **51**, 52–53
  maps **51**, **54**, **55**
Fort Lamy (now N'Djamena) 38
forts, Italian **4**, 33
French forces, the 7, 10
French forces: *compagnies sahariennes* 14
French forces, Free (Forces Françaises Libres – FFL) 7, 8, 24, 37, **38**, **40**, 50
  Colonne Leclerc see Colonne Leclerc
  command structure 76, 77
  Compagnie portée of Capitaine de Renneport 53, 57
  doctrine 13
  at Kufra 53, **56**, 57, **58**
  Légion étrangère (French Foreign Legion) 38
  Patrouille A 61, 63, 64
  Patrouille D 61, 63, 64
  raid in the Fezzan 61, **62**, 63–64
  Régiment de tirailleurs sénégalais du Tchad (RTST, later Colonne Leclerc) 38, **39**, 39, **56**
    12e compagnie 63, 64
  Groupe nomade de l'Ennedi (GNE) 38, 39, 53
  Groupe nomade du Borkou (GNB) 38, 41, 44
  Groupe nomade du Tibesti (GNT) 38, 41, 44, 63
  unit organization 38–44
    see also Colonne Leclerc: organization
Fuka landing ground 75

Gatrun 44, 52, 63–64
Gazala Line 47, 67
German forces
  Abwehr (intelligence service) 47–48, 73
    Sonderkommando von Almaszy 48, 48, **73**, **74**, 74, **87**

Afrika Division, 90.: 75
Kampfgruppe Hecker 46, 47
leadership 77–78
Luftwaffe **74**, 74
Pionier Landungs Kompanie 778: 47
Sonderkommando Dora 34, **45**, 48–49, **49**, **78**
  vehicles 85–86
Sonderverband (Special Formation) 288 (later Panzer Grenadier Regiment Afrika) 45, 45–46, **46**
  Kampfgruppe Menton 45–47
  13./Lehr Regiment Brandenburg (aka Tropen Kompanie) 46–47, **47**, 49, 74
  unit organization 45–49
  Verband Homeyer 45
Gurdon, Lt. 75

Hagfet Gelgaf 67
Haselden, Lt. Col. J. E. 71
Hon 44

Indian Army, Long Range Desert Squadron (Indian Long Range Squadron – ILRS) 23, 24
intelligence 80–81
Iraqi rebellion 14
Italian forces **7**, 8, 9, **27**, 37, 50, 67, 72, 89
  see also Libyan forces
  Arditi, 10a 87, **88**
  Arditi companies 12, 37
  Aviazione Sahariana **9**, **52**
  Battaglione Sahariano 27–28
  Carabinieri (military police) 52
  colonna mobile 52–53, 57
  Comando del Sahara Libico 28, 30, 31, 33–34, 76–77
    organization (Dec. 1940) **29**
    organization (Aug. 1941) **30**
    organization (Feb. 1942) **30**
    organization (Oct. 1942) **35**, **36**
  Comando Fronte Sud (Southern Front Command) (later Comando del Sahara Libico) 27, 28
  command structure 76
  communications 80
  Compagnie Libice da Posizione **33**, 34, 84
  Compagnia Mista Genio del Sahara Libico (Libyan Sahara Mixed Engineers Company) 80
  Compagnie Mitraglieri de Posizione (later *Compagnie Libice*) **26**, 27, 28, 31, **33**, 57, 83
    57a Compagnia 50, 52
  Compagnie Meharisti 27, **28**, 31, 33
    1ª Compagnia 63, 64
  Compagnie Sahariane (Auto-Saharan companies) 10, 12, 14, 37, 50, 52, 80, 81, 84
    3ª and 4ª Compagnie 64
    organization 27, 28, 30, 33
    organization (1940) **28**, **29**
    organization (25 March 1942) **34**, **35**
  doctrine 9, 10–11, 12–13
  Gruppo Cammellato Tuareg 27
  'mobile column' 33
  motorised column 75
  officers **6**, **33**
  Pattuglia Vigilanza Terrestre Avanzata (advanced land surveillance patrol) 37
  'Pavia' Division 75
  Polizia dell'Africa Italiana (PAI) **31**, 34, 37, **76**
  Raggruppamento Maletti (Battlegroup Maletti) 28

Raggruppamento Mannerini (aka Raggruppamento Sahariano) 37
Raggruppamento Sahariano 13
Reparto Celere (fast-moving unit) 3: 37
San Marco Regiment 71
Squadre di Pilotaggio Zone Desertiche (desert navigation schools) 37
'Trieste' Division 75
unit organization 26–37
Italian forts 4, 33
Italians 6

Jalo Oasis 70, 71–72, 74
Jebel Akhdar 60, 61, 67, 81
Jebel Sherif 52, 81

Kalansho Sand Sea 6, 74
Kennedy-Shaw, Lt William B. 14, 15
Kitchener, Gen. 9
Kufra 18, 19, 24, 27, 41, 50, 78
Free French forces at 53, **56**, 57, **58**

landing strips 9
Lawrence, Col. Thomas Edward ('Lawrence of Arabia') 7, 9, 14
Leclerc, Col. Philippe (Viscount Philippe de Hauteclocque) 13, 38–39, 41, 41, 44, 53, 57, 64, 78
see also Colonne Leclerc
Libya 10
Libyan Desert 6
see also Western Desert
Libyan forces 10, 26–27, 30
see also Italian forces
Meharisti units 6, 11, 12, 13
Meharisti del Fezzan units 27, 27, 28
mortar team 32
'sahariana' companies 10
soldiers 9, 10, 31
Lloyd Owen, David 22
Long Range Desert Group (LRDG) 8, 14, **15**, 18, 39, 41, 57, **60**, **61**, 89
artillery section (Heavy Section) 18, 84
command 77, 78–79
communications 79–80
control 77
doctrine 11, 13
in the Fezzan 50, **51**, 52–53, **54**, **55**
HQ 18, 20, 22, 24, 77, 78, 79
intelligence 80–81
New Zealanders 14, 14–15, 16, 72
in Operation Crusader 20, 21–22
organization 16–24
Dec. 1940–Jan. 1941 **17**
Mar.–Apr. 1941 **19**
June 1941 **20**
Oct. 1941 **21**
Feb. 1942 **23**, 24
June–July 1942 **25**
Oct. 1942 **26**
T Patrol, Dec. 1940–Mar. 1941 **18**
patrols 7
G Patrol 16, 19, 50, 52, 57, 60, **61**, **71**
G1 Patrol 72, 75
G2 Patrol 67, 75
H Patrol 18–19, 60
I1 and I2 Patrols 23
I3 and I4 Patrols 24
R Patrol 61
R1 Patrol 22, 66
R2 Patrol 67
S Patrol 16–17, 61
S1 Patrol 22, 66, 67
S2 Patrol 67
T Patrol 15, **18**, 50, 52, 60–61, **71**

T1 Patrol 67, 72, 75
Y Patrol 18, 19, **22**
Y1 Patrol 70
Y2 Patrol 67, 72, 75
portée **53**
raids in Egypt **72**, 72, **73**, 75
reconnaissance in Cyrenaica and Tripolitania 57, **59**, 60–61
'road-watching' 61, **80**, 81
SAS joint operations 22, 23, 24, 64, **65**, 66–67, 70, 71
specializations breakdown 11–12
squadrons
A Squadron 18, 19, 20, 21, 22, 23, 57, 60
A Squadron (MEC) 23, 24
B Squadron 18, 21, 22–23
C Squadron (MEC) 23, 24, 67
training 11

Mannerini, Gen. Alberto 37
Mayne, Lt. 66
McCraith, Capt. P. J. D. 18
Menton, Obst. Otto 45
Mersa Sciausc 70–71
Mitford, Capt. E. C. 15, 79
Murray, Gen. Archibald 14
Murzuk 50, 52, **53**

N'Djamena (formerly Fort Lamy) 38
New Zealanders 14, 14–15, 16, 72

O'Connor, Lt. Gen. Richard 50
oases 7, 9, 10, 11
officers, Italian **6**, 33
Operation
Agreement **70**, 70–71, **71**
Bigamy 70, 71
Caravan 70, 71, 72
Compass 28, 50
Condor 48, 74
Crusader 20, 21–22
Nicety 70, 71–72
Salaam 48, 73–74, **87**
organization, unit 14–49
British forces see British forces: unit organization; Long Range Desert Group: organization
Free French forces see Colonne Leclerc: organization; French forces, Free: unit organization
German forces see German forces, unit organization
Italian forces see Italian forces, unit organization

Pasha, el Masri 73–74
Peniakoff, Maj. Vladimir 'Popski' 81
see also British forces: 'Popski's Private Army'
Piatti Dal Pozzo, Gen. Umberto 30, 33, 34, 37, 77, 78
Prendergast, Lt. Col. Guy L. 14, 15, 19, 78, 79

radio communications 79–80
Rémy, Cdt. 44
Ribiana Sand Sea 6
Ritter, Maj. Nikolaus 48
Rommel, Gen. Erwin 30, 45, 47, 57, 67, 70, 74

Senussi tribe 9, 10, 81
Sidi Barrani 28
Sikh, HMS 70, 71
Sirte airstrip 22
Siwa Oasis 7, 14, 21, 22, 24, 61
Slonta 67
Steele, Capt. D. G. 15, 79
Stirling, Col. David 22, 66, 71, 75, 78, 88

tactics 50–75
big raids, Sept. 1942 67, **68**, **69**, 70–72
Fezzan, first campaign in 61, **62**, 63–64
Free French at Kufra 53, **56**, 57, **58**
LRDG in the Fezzan 50, **51**, 52–53, **54**, **55**
LRDG raids in Egypt **72**, 72, **73**, 75
LRDG reconnaissance in Cyrenaica and Tripolitania 57, **59**, 60–61
LRDG/SAS partnership 64, **65**, 66–67, 70, 71
Tamet airstrip 66
Tibesti Mountains 6
Tobruk 70–71
Tragen 52
Tripoli 44, 48, 61, **73**
Tripolitania, reconnaissance in 57, **59**, 60–61

'Ultra' intelligence 81
Um el Araneb 44, 52, 64

vehicles 10, 84–87
armoured cars 9
SPA AB41 **76**
car, Fiat 500 Coloniale 37
German forces 48, 78
Sonderkommando Dora 85–86
von Almaszy's **74**, 74
Italian forces 86–87
jeep, Willys **66**, **71**, 85
Kübelwagen **45**, 48, 86
LRDG 84–85
motorcycles 34, **76**
trucks
Bedford 40
Chevrolet 15-cwt 20
Chevrolet WB 30-cwt 14, **15**, 15, **22**, 23, **53**
Fiat/SPA Autocarro Sahariano AS37 3-ton **7**, **37**, **75**, **86**, 86
Ford **87**
Ford F30 30-cwt 20, **22**, 23
Ford Marmon-Herrington 15
Ford V8 15-cwt 15
Mack 10-ton 23
SPA/Viberti AS42 Sahariana **7**, 12, **37**, 37, **84**, 86–87, **88**
TL37 **56**, **63**
Via Balbia 34, 47, 81
von Almaszy, Count Ladislas 'Lazlo' Edouard (formerly de Almaszy) 5, 48, **73**, 73–74, **74**, 77, **87**
von Homeyer, Hptm. 45
von Leipzig, Oblt. Conrad 48

Wavell, Lt. Gen. Sir Archibald 14, 78
weapons 82–84
Bofors gun, 37mm 53
British forces
Long Range Desert Group 82, 83–84
Long Range Desert Patrols 15
gun, 47/32 **84**
gun, Breda M35 20mm dual-purpose **82**
Italian 31, 33, 34, 82–83, 84, 87
machine gun, 7.5mm light 40
machine gun, Breda 30 6.5mm light 10, 12
machine gun, Hotchkiss 40
mortar, 81mm 32
musket, 91/38 12
rifle, Mannlicher Carcano Model 91/24 6.5mm **6**, 12
sabotage equipment 83
submachine gun, Beretta 38 9mm **76**
Western Desert **5**
see also Libyan Desert

Zulu, HMS 70, 71